THIN MINT MEMORIES

THIN MINT

Memories

SCOUTING FOR EMPOWERMENT
THROUGH THE
GIRL SCOUT COOKIE PROGRAM

Shelley Johnson Carey

Shelley Johnson Carey, Author
www.shelleyjohnsoncarey.com

Clear Message Press
Carole C. Hayward, Publisher
www.clearmessagemedia.org/press

Michele Stinson, Cover design

Gessert Books, Book design, typesetting, and typography

ISBN 0998148008

Print: 978-0-9981480-0-7
E-book: 978-0-9981480-1-4

Contents

ACKNOWLEDGMENTS

Make New Friends but Keep the Old

As I became acquainted with the wonderful leader who allowed me to shadow her troop, the girls in the troop who let me eavesdrop on their conversations, and the parents who let me have a peek at their lives, I can say that Girl Scouting provides the same benefits for today's girls as it did for me. Obtaining initial access to a troop was harder than I thought it would be. But I was truly fortunate that my pleading email landed in Jennifer M.'s inbox. From the first time I told her about the project, she made it possible for me to see for myself what Girl Scouts are like in the twenty-first century. In the two years that I observed this troop, my admiration for her, the girls in the troop, and their parents grew with every interaction. I saw how, mostly through cookie sales, the troop funded a range of activities that gave them a strong foundation of skills, emotional well-being, practical knowledge, and self-sufficiency. And while girl drama was still part of their world, thanks to their scouting experiences and the adults like Jennifer, the troop members became capable and confident young women.

I want to acknowledge Julie Carlson, the product sales manager for the Girl Scouts Council of the Nation's Capital, from whom I learned much of what I now know about the Girl Scout cookie program on the council level. I am also grateful to Yevgeniya Gribov, Archivist for the Girl Scouts of the USA, for her generous support in helping me research many aspects of this project and to Kathryn White, Advisor at the Juliette Gordon Low Birthplace, for additional research assistance. Michelle Tompkins, former Girl Scouts of the USA National Spokesperson, and her colleagues were also instrumental in helping me gain a national perspective on the Girl Scout cookie program. I am indebted to Connie L. Lindsey, former President of the Girl Scouts of the USA, for sending me her thoughts on Girl Scouts and her memories of her own cookie sales.

I thank my Goucher College mentors, Laura Wexler, Leslie Rubinkowski, Tom French, and Diana Hume George for their patience and guidance in helping me develop and write this manuscript. Many thanks also to those who shared their "Thin Mint Memories" that are sprinkled throughout these pages—Robyn Barberry, Jill Brodsky, Carole Hayward, Christy Hepburn, Emily Epstein Landau, Patricia Marshall, Lisa McPherson, Brian Mockenhaupt, Martha Moore, Pamela Myrick, Dede Neufeld, Nancy O'Neill, Beth Ramage, Monica Snipes, Danita Ferguson Terry, and Tabitha Whissemore.

I also owe a debt of gratitude to my colleagues at the Association of American Colleges and Universities for their support and to my family and friends for their steadfast encouragement to keep going when it seemed easier to stop.

Finally, I am indebted to my husband, Tony, and my children, Lauren, Gillian, and Adam, for their love, understanding, and sustenance. Very special thanks go to Gwendolyn Bacoats Johnson for being a wonderful mother and Girl Scout leader and for sharing her own Girl Scout memories with me.

The Girl Scout Path to Empowerment Is Paved with Cookies

Selling cookies was, for me, one of the most fun and rewarding experiences in Girl Scouting. My "career" as a Girl Scout began when I was 11 years old, at my church in Milwaukee, Wisconsin. I started in Girl Scouts as a Junior and my involvement has continued into adulthood. The power of the Girl Scout Promise and Law live inside of me and has empowered me to pursue and achieve my goals and to be of service to others.

Connie L. Lindsey
Former President, Girl Scouts of the USA (2008-2014)

W ho doesn't love Girl Scout cookies? Even that rare breed of man or woman born without a sweet tooth can't say no to the breathless sales pitches of snaggle-toothed Brownies or the pleading eyes of Junior Scouts swathed in badges. Girl Scout cookies are as much of the American experience as hot dogs and baseball. As someone commented in an online blog, "If you don't buy Girl Scout cookies—that's un-American!"

While there *are* reported to be individuals who can resist small uniformed girls in khaki and green *and* the allure of Thin Mints, the majority of Americans cannot. We're hooked on those little cookies. So much so that Girl Scout cookie business is big business—nearly 200 million boxes are sold every year. Priced at an average of $4.50 a box, the annual national gross sales of cookies is nearly $800 million. Cookie sales fund almost all of the educational programs and leadership activities for 112 regional Girl Scout councils and for 236,000+ individual troops and affiliated groups. And since Girl Scout cookies are only available for a few months every year, true fans put the cookie sales season on their foodie indulgence calendars along with Halloween, Thanksgiving, and Christmas.

The idea to write about Girl Scout cookies came to me through a classroom writing exercise. The instructions were to figure out what kind of geek you were when you were growing up and write about it. It didn't take me long to remember my geekiness—in the 60s and 70s when most kids my age were rebelling against the establishment, I was a Girl Scout. True, I was a stealth Scout—I didn't wear my uniform to school—but I stayed active until my junior year of high school and probably would have gone on until the end if the other girls in my troop hadn't dropped out. And while being a Scout didn't necessarily make me popular, all of the kids in my school sought me out when it was time to buy Girl Scout cookies.

My love for Girl Scout cookies continued when I was a nineteen-year-old Girl Scout camp counselor. One day instead of the usual vanilla pudding or strawberry Jell-O, we were treated to a new kind of cookie for dessert—the Samoa. While I had indulged in classic Girl Scout cookies that you can never go wrong with—cool crisp Thin Mints and rich buttery Trefoils—the cookies of my youth were not nearly as scrumptious to me as this new variety. On top of the donut-shaped cookie was a thick layer of golden caramel and flaky coconut, topped with chocolate stripes. With each bite, the caramel stretched as it separated from the cookie base. The coconut provided a satisfying chewy sensation. The chocolate was rich and flavorful without overwhelming the other tastes. Under the trees of Camp May Flather, I'd found a passion that would outlast my love for disco and polyester bell bottoms. To have and to hold, from this day forward, forever and ever—let no man, woman, or child come between me and my Samoa cookies.

Earlier in my scouting days, my mother, who was also my Girl Scout leader, took on the added role of "Cookie Depot" Mom for a couple of years. The Cookie Depot was the place where the Cookie Moms from individual troops came to pick up their orders. With more than twenty troops in our area, our Cookie Depot was the site of a heck of a lot of cookies. For at least a few days every year, our family room was jam-packed with hundreds of cookie cartons. The cookies arrived by moving van and the guys who delivered them neatly stacked so many brown cardboard cartons up against the walls that our house looked like a cookie fortress. Inside of each carton were twelve boxes of peanut butter, vanilla shortbread, chocolate mint, or sandwich cookies. For that short while every year I lived in a cookie wonderland.

Selling cookies was nothing new to my mother, Gwendolyn Bacoats Johnson. In 1938, as a senior Girl Scout in Oklahoma, she sold shortbreads in one of the first national cookie drives. At that time, the significance of that sale was not something she thought about. Her source of pride centered on the fact that she had been chosen to be part of the first African American Girl Scout troop in Tulsa.

"Our leader, Miss Lithcott, the dean of women at George Washington Carver Junior High, had been selected to receive an official troop charter from the National Office," my mother said. "You couldn't be a real troop without a charter. Then she handpicked the girls that she wanted in Scouts. That was back in about 1936. Girl Scouts were ahead of the rest of the country when it came to including everyone."

The railroad tracks that divided north from south Tulsa also marked the line of segregation in the city. Black residents lived in the north and white residents lived in the southern part of the city. And the two did not mix or interact. Ever. That unspoken rule had been agreed upon back in 1921 when Tulsa experienced what many historians call the worst race riot of the twentieth century. Before the race riot, Tulsa was already segregated but without the undercurrent of animosity that existed afterward. So the girls in my mother's troop sold as many cookies as they could on their side of tracks.

In 1938, talking anyone into buying cookies wasn't easy—it was at the end of the Great Depression. "We wrote down our orders in a book, so people had to order their cookies in advance," my mother recalls. "Then, a month or so later, we went back to deliver them. Sometimes when we went back to deliver the cookies, people would say, 'Sorry, I can't afford them anymore.' I guess my mother bought all of the cookies that I couldn't sell. I was lucky that we had the money to buy them. Those were hard times."

Selling cookies not only allowed my mother to help raise funds for her troop's activities, but it also gave her a better sense of the world that she otherwise wouldn't have known. The personal growth she experienced and the ability to empathize and recognize inequities are as much of what scouting is about now as it was when my mother was a Girl Scout and when Juliette Gordon Low founded the organization in 1912.

Juliette Low, or Daisy, as Girl Scouts remember her, was a visionary who appreciated and advocated for women to stretch themselves far beyond the limited roles they were assigned in the early twentieth century. By the time women finally got the right to vote in 1920, Low's Girl Scouts were ready for almost any challenge. The first Girl Scout Handbook gave girls concrete information about a then taboo subject, menstruation, explained Morse Code, offered recipes for beef stew, and gave instructions on how to identify mad dogs and poisonous snakes. Low's American girls were smart and prepared, then and now. Girl Scout Founders Day is celebrated on October 31, Low's birthday. Halloween also happens to be my birthday. While I think I would have chosen to write about this subject without our sharing a birthday, it is one more connection that I feel with Girl Scouts.

Whenever I read a book, I wonder what made the author choose to write about that subject. After all, it takes years to complete researching and writing a book. So to maintain the quality of the story and the interest of the readers, the author must feel passion for the subject matter. When I first chose to write a social/cultural history of Girl Scout cookies and their iconic value, I thought I would simply write about the cookies. Without a doubt, I felt passionate about Samoas.

A bit into the writing process, after getting to know some junior high and high school age Girl Scouts and by trying to remember my own adolescence, I realized that the story I wanted to tell had more depth than the cookies themselves. Then it came to me why cookies and scouting meant so much to me. Besides helping me to sharpen fundamental leadership skills, scouting also provided support for me at a critical time. When I was fifteen, after a long illness, my father died. Looking back, I realize that Girl Scouts and its traditions provided me with an emotional anchor at a time when both my family and school life were dizzying. So my Thin Mint Memories are about more than cookie sales. Many of these memories are an appreciative nod to the ways that Girl Scouts touched and formed me.

The first three chapters of this book are meant to relay historical information. Then I present the council-level view. Chapter 6-10 allow the reader to experience the girl/troop perspective, and finally the last two chapters have a national focus. While every sales season brings new challenges and rewards to troops in the many Girl Scout councils, I hope that the universal events presented here will provide more understanding to those who have never experienced selling Girl Scout cookies and bring a sense of recognition to those who have.

Selling cookies was one of the ways I learned the importance of financial discipline. While it was not evident then, I was developing leadership skills and financial acumen every time I delivered a box of cookies to a satisfied customer. I learned the importance of goal setting and the power of persuasion and public speaking. Today, the Girl Scout cookie program is the largest girl-led business in the country—to a tune of [nearly $800 million a year in revenue for our girls and communities nationwide. I'm proud to have been—and still be—a part of this wonderful program. We teach our girls the merits of financial literacy—millions of girls now learn their economic ABCs in Girl Scouts: setting goals, budgeting, and saving. Furthermore, no university has produced as many female business owners as has the Girl Scout cookie program!

Connie L. Lindsey

"Every cookie has a mission." So began a public service announcement on YouTube that was created a few years ago for the Girl Scout cookie program. The video explains how selling cookies is more than a money-making venture for the girls. Using animated cookies, the video furthers its message this way: "This cookie helps train girls in CPR. This cookie cheers up our soldiers around the world. This cookie teaches girls how to set goals and manage money. Every cookie has a mission!"

When I thought about the major themes of this work, a mental image came to mind. It was similar to the Yellow Brick Road from the *Wizard of Oz,* but this path was made out of Girl Scout cookies—Thin Mints, Samoas, Do-Si-Dos, Trefoils—all of the favorites. Skipping down that path was the long green line of Girl Scouts through the ages. Those girls, past and present, were guided by "cookies on a mission" toward life skills for empowerment—blended with friendship and fun—for them all. ❧

"My family integrated our New Jersey neighborhood and not everyone was nice to us. There always seems to be a real curmudgeon on every block, and ours was Mrs. Rizzo—not only was she mean to me, most of the time she was unpleasant to everyone. In Mrs. Rizzo's defense, she did live next door to the Donoghues, who had six boys, so she may have had reason to be a bit grumpy. When I began selling Girl Scout cookies, I expected many of my neighbors to ignore my sales calls, especially Mrs. Rizzo. To my surprise, I was wrong about her. Every year she would come to the gate, let me in her house, and invite me to sit in her kitchen. Mrs. Rizzo would look at the order card over and over again, but she always limited her purchase to just three boxes of sugar shortbread cookies. That type of sale experience really boosted my self-confidence. I knew that no matter what I looked like, I was selling an excellent product and I presented myself well. I believe that kind of confidence follows you. In addition to selling Girl Scout cookies, I began selling greeting cards door-to-door, too. Eventually I gained enough self-confidence that I spent several years as a runway model. By selling Girl Scout cookies, I learned to keep going despite the real and proverbial doors that shut in my face because I knew that there were always other doors that would open wide to new and exciting possibilities."

Danita Ferguson Terry

"Around age 6, I decided I wanted a horse of my own. My horse obsession reached its peak when I wrote and illustrated my own miniature book called *My Horse, Sunset*. By the time I turned 8 and joined my school's Junior Girl Scout troop, I was ready to leave upstate New York and move to a ranch in the mythical West.

One day my troop leader announced we were going to use some of our cookie sales proceeds to earn a badge in horseback riding. When the troop arrived at the stable, we were buzzing with excitement. After what seemed like hours, the stable owner and our troop leader each led a horse to the outside pen. It was then that I confronted reality. The horses were gigantic. They snorted and kicked at the ground with their hooves. After my troop leader boosted me up to get into the saddle. I looked down, and the ground seemed to be a mile away. Afterward, when my mom asked how it went, I said "good," afraid that if I said more I would cry.

Being a Girl Scout provided me with reality testing. It is one thing to have a romanticized notion about something, but it is something else entirely to put one's own foot in the stirrup. This was true for riding a horse, pitching a tent, and fashioning a sling from a handkerchief. Earning a badge in all of these different areas represented experience, and from that experience, learning. I learned about myself as I learned about the world around me."

Nancy O'Neill

PART ONE

Girl Scout History

Before the Cookies — The Juliette Low Story

"Come right over, I've got something for the girls of Savannah, and all America, and all the world, and we're going to start it tonight!"

From the time they are the youngest Daisies, just beginning their scouting adventures, all Girl Scouts hear and memorize the legendary story of how Juliette Low, the group's founder, made an eager call to her cousin and proclaimed that the time had come to start the first American troop (initially called Girl Guides) on the historic night of March 12, 1912. Funding this new group by selling her wedding pearls, Low's Girl Scouts endured to become the influential organization that it is today. Juliette Low's vision of a group that would teach girls the skills to empower them to become creative and capable adults came before American women had even gained the right to vote.

As the narrator of this story, I will not editorialize much, but I want to say up front how wonderful I think this woman was. Many legends, when you pull back the gauzy filters, fail to live up to their reputations. When you learn the full story of Juliette Low (which I found by scouring the Girl Scouts' archives), you can't help but admire her wholeheartedly. The inside story of this woman may lack the romance of the fabled tale that Scouts have passed down through the years, but it celebrates the spirit and strength of a woman who had much to overcome.

Juliette Magill Kinzie Gordon was the second of six children born to her parents, William Washington Gordon and Eleanor Kinzie Gordon. She made her appearance on October 31, 1860, in Savannah, Georgia, only months before the beginning of the Civil War. From the time she was a baby, everyone called her Daisy. This nickname was given to her by her uncle who thought she looked as fresh as a field of spring flowers. The name suited her, so friends and strangers called her Daisy for the rest of her life.

During the Civil War, Baby Daisy's mother packed up her belongings, and she and the children relocated to Chicago where they lived with her parents. Daisy's father, meanwhile, served as a Captain in the Confederate army. Once the war ended, the Gordon family returned to Savannah, and Captain Gordon remained there until he was, much later, commissioned as a General of the local volunteer militia who fought in the Spanish American War. During his service during the Civil War, he returned home periodically to rest and recover, often leaving Daisy's mother with child.

From childhood, Daisy suffered from hearing problems, which some say came from a brain fever she came down with as a baby and others attribute to constant ear infections. Her health didn't stop her from going to school. She was a bright, curious girl who loved to read and sculpt. To further Daisy's education, her parents sent her to the best boarding schools they could find—the Virginia Female Institute and Mesdemoiselles Charbonniers, an exclusive French finishing school in New York City. During school vacations, she filled up her family home with pets.

Young Daisy was an advocate for all types of creatures and it is rumored that she constantly came home with stray dogs, cats, and even horses. Because she was such an animal advocate, one year Daisy came up with what she thought would be a more humane way for her family to celebrate Thanksgiving. In his 1956 *Woman's Day* article, "My Aunt Daisy was the First Girl Scout," Juliette's nephew, Arthur Gordon, wrote about the time when, as a child, Daisy Gordon talked her family into giving their turkey what she thought would be a more compassionate demise. She convinced her family that decapitation was inhumane and argued that the bird could be chloroformed first, and then it wouldn't feel anything. Her family decided to go along with Daisy's plan. After the bird had been anesthetized, they plucked it and put the turkey into the icebox. When they opened it the next day, the bird was wide awake and bolted from its frozen cage. The cook, thinking the bird was dead, became hysterical and jumped on top of the stove.

In her young adult years, Juliette was fairly content with her life, but her health was always a concern. At twenty-five, Juliette came down with another ear infection. After hearing about a new treatment—silver nitrate—that had been used by other patients with similar ear problems, her doctor put drops of the chemical in her ear, in hopes of finding a cure. Instead of fixing the problem, however, the silver nitrate permanently damaged her eardrum.

The next year on December 21, 1886, her parents' twenty-sixth wedding anniversary, Juliette "Daisy" Gordon married William "Willy" Mackay Low, a British merchandizing heir, whose mother had been raised in Savannah. After the ceremony, as the new bride and groom were leaving the church, a grain from the rice that guests threw for good luck found its way into her "bad" ear. Because she was leaving for her honeymoon, she was not able to see a doctor for many months. The rice festered in her ear and caused an infection. When it was finally removed, the instrument the doctor used made her nearly deaf in that ear.

In her book, *Juliette Gordon Low: The Remarkable Founder of the Girl Scouts,* Stacey Cordery theorizes that Low's hearing in her other "good" ear deteriorated due to sympathetic hearing loss and "general ill health." Within a year of her marriage, Juliette Low had very poor hearing in both ears.

The newlyweds moved to England, where they remained for the rest of their marriage. Once they were settled, William Low commissioned Edward Hughes, a talented artist who had created works of the Royal Family and much of European High Society, to paint the portrait of his new bride that now holds a place of honor in the National Portrait Gallery in Washington, DC. In the large work, the new bride is luminous in a pale apricot brocade dress adorned with delicate, translucent sleeves and she holds a white ostrich feather fan on her lap. A large bustle juts out behind her as she sits in an outdoor setting that is neither sunny nor stormy. Thick clouds billow in the background as she seems to contemplate the life before her. Juliette Gordon Low shows not a hint of a smile, preferring to strike a solemn pose in this image that captured her twenty-seventh year.

Although the Lows were married for nearly nineteen years, their marriage became strained years before its demise. Although Daisy loved children and hoped to have a family with her husband, their marriage remained childless. Another issue that may have caused strain between the couple was Daisy's constant travels to the United States. While her father served in the Spanish American War, Juliette helped her mother care for wounded soldiers coming back from Cuba. Willy's drinking increased, and it became clear to Juliette that her husband's attention and affections were not with her. In 1901, Juliette decided to file for a divorce. Before the divorce proceedings could be finalized, her husband suffered a stroke and died in 1905.

When his will was read, Juliette discovered that her husband had left most of his money to his mistress. She was left only with a small widow's pension. She contested his will and eventually won a $500,000 settlement. Even with the money and the freedom it afforded her, she felt heartbroken and depressed about the way her marriage had ended, so she spent the next several years traveling through Europe and India, without roots. In her travels, Juliette met Lord Robert Baden-Powell, the founder of British Boy Scouts and his sister Agnes, who formed similar groups for British girls. In 1909, Robert Baden-Powell published a two-part set of pamphlets called *Baden-Powell Girl Guides, a Suggestion for Character Training for Girls*. These were precursors to the handbook. By April 1910, there were 6,000 young girls registered as Girl Guides. The brother and sister introduced Juliette to the basics of scouting, and she felt as though she had found meaning to her life. With Agnes's help, she started a troop of Girl Guides in Scotland and then two more in London.

In 1912, Juliette Low moved back to the United States to live in the Low family house. It was from there that she made the famous phone call that brought Girl Scouting to the United States.

Let's stop now to assess everything that went wrong for this champion of girls' opportunity. At the lowest point of her life when depression could have set in because she as a woman with a hearing impairment who was widowed and impoverished (okay, she wasn't destitute once she received her settlement, but still...), Juliette Low did not give up on life but found a new way to embrace it. While most would certainly agree that the story of a drinking, cheating husband has no place in the Girl Scout story shared with Daisies and Brownies, once you know the full details of this triumphant story, it's hard not to admire Juliette Daisy Gordon Low that much more for having the fortitude—in the face of adversity—to bring Girl Scouts to the United States.

So now we're back to the point in the story where we began. Once she made the call to her cousin and brought girls together to form the first troop, the rest of the Juliette Low's Girl Scout story, though less dramatic, is also inspirational. She gathered eighteen high school girls to register the first troop of American Girl Guides. To raise the funds needed to keep the troop going, legend says that Juliette Low sold the pearls that she'd received as a wedding present from her husband. That was one of life's sweetest revenges, I think—to take a gift from the man who tried to cheat her out of her inheritance and use it to fund an organization that would empower many generations of young women.

Margaret "Daisy Doots" Gordon, her niece and namesake, was the first registered member. The name of the group was changed to Girl Scouts the following year. The organization was incorporated in 1915, with Juliette serving as president until 1920 when she was granted the title of founder.

Photographs of a weathered Juliette Low taken during her time leading the Girl Scouts show that the events of her earlier life had their effects on the young bride who sat for her oil portrait in England. However, she was known for being charming but eccentric. She was known to wear a watch with only one hand, saying, "The fact that it only had one hand, and couldn't really tell the time, never really bothered me."

Juliette also used her deafness to her advantage. She was a tireless fundraiser for the Girl Scouts, and in that role, she felt comfortable asking anyone to make large donations of their time or money to the organization. She never took no for an answer. When anyone responded negatively, she acted as though she misunderstood them and thanked them gratefully for their generous support.

Her nephew also recalled how, at one of the first Girl Scout board meetings, she stood on her head to display the new Girl Scout shoes that she was wearing. Throughout her life, Low continued to sketch, write, and act in plays; and she became a skilled painter and sculptor. Her love of pets endured, and she became particularly fond of exotic birds and Georgia mockingbirds. She was also known for her poetic writing as demonstrated by her New Year's Message by Juliette Low published in the January 1919 issue of *Rally* magazine:

> *Did you ever think how wonderful it is that with every new Spring sap should rise in the trees? No one knows whence it comes, but it flows from root to branch, and makes a dead bare tree blossom with green leaves....And so it is with scouting, it rises within you and inspires you to put forth your best.*

For fifteen years, Juliette Low devoted her time, energy, and finances to the Girl Scout movement. She was never hesitant to ask for major support and contributions from communities and businesses, big and small. In an effort to expand the Girl Scouts, Low attempted to merge the group with the likeminded Campfire Girls, but this fell through because of administrative disputes. She oversaw the composition of the Girl Scout handbook, *How Girls Can Help Their Country*, and Juliette Low was the representative at the first international meeting of Girl Scouts and Guides in 1919.

The Girl Scouts celebrate Juliette every year on her birthday—Halloween—with Founders Day activities. To mark the occasion, she published a birthday letter in *The Rally*, the official Scout magazine. In her 1925 letter, she wrote:

> *Dear Girl Scouts,*
> *Your editor has suggested that perhaps I might tell you what Girl Scouting means to me. I wish that I might. Yet I find that I cannot put it into adequate words all that Girl Scouting has meant to me. I realize that each year it has changed and grown until I know that, a decade from now, what I might say of it would seem like an echo of what has been instead of what is.*

Juliette Gordon Low was diagnosed with breast cancer in 1923, but she kept her illness a secret from most of her family and friends, while she continued diligently working for the Girl Scouts. Low died January 17, 1927, and was buried in her Girl Scout uniform in Laurel Grove Cemetery in Savannah.

Today, there are 3.3 million Girl Scouts of the United States of America—2.4 million girl members and 928,000 adult members. Girls at home and abroad participate in more than 236,000 troops and groups in more than 90 countries through USA Girl Scouts Overseas. From the time that Juliette Low founded the Girl Scouts until today, the group's mission statement has endeavored to capture the essence of her vision:

1912—To train girls to take their rightful places in life, first as good women, then as good citizens, wives, and mothers.

1917—To promote, through organization and co-operation with other agencies, the virtues of womanhood, by training girls to recognize their obligations to God and Country, to prepare for the duties devolving upon women in the home, in society and the state, and to guide others in ways conducive to personal honor and the public good.

1924—To help girls to realize the ideals of womanhood as a preparation for their responsibilities in the home and service to the community.

1953—The Girl Scout organization is dedicated to helping girls develop as happy, resourceful individuals willing to share their abilities as citizens in their homes, their communities, their country and the world.

The current mission statement is shorter than most that came before, but in a few select words the group's message returns to the basics principles that Low had in mind when she called that first group of girls together in 1912.

Present day—Girl Scouting builds girls of courage, confidence, and character, who make the world a better place!

Juliette Low, when explaining the meaning of the Girl Scout badges in a letter published in the October 1925 *American Girl* magazine, expressed it in a way that still resonates nearly a century later:

Every badge you earn is tied up to your motto. This badge is not a reward for something you have done once or for an examination you have passed. Badges are not medals to wear on your sleeve to show what a smart girl you are. A badge is a symbol that you have done the thing it stands for often enough, thoroughly enough, and well enough to BE PREPARED to give service in it. You wear the badge to let people know that you are prepared and willing to be called on because you are a Girl Scout. And Girl Scouting is not just knowing...but doing...not just doing, but being.

Juliette Low's legacy is an organization that has changed with the times to remain relevant to teens of different eras. However, the basic tenets of the Girl Scouts of the USA—girl empowerment—remain the same. ❧

"When my daughter was interested in joining her best friend's Brownie troop, there was only one opening and a couple of little girls vying for the spot. The leaders shared with me that, if I were willing to step into one of the leadership roles, then that could tip things in my daughter's favor. One of those roles was Troop Cookie Manager.

I immediately flashed back 30 years to when I was a Girl Scout and my own sagas of selling cookies. I always enjoyed it, even when there was drama, like the time I didn't turn in my order form on time and my order had to be pieced together from booth sale inventory.

I've since become more organized and thought that taking on that role was something I could do to give back to the Girl Scouts and help my daughter. It was a great experience! I enjoyed working with the girls to teach them about sales, safety, motivation, and reaching their goals. And we had a lot of fun doing it.

Despite having hundreds of boxes of cookies in my garage and having to keep track of all the money involved, I enjoyed it all. So the next year, when the leaders told me that my name came up for District Cookie Manager, I accepted.

My daughter is grown now, but I still smile when I see the 'I can't survive without Girl Scout Cookies and a little help from my friends at the Girl Scout Council of the Nation's Capital' coffee mug that I received as a thank you."

Carole Hayward

"I was a shy kid. Around my family, I could talk a mile a minute. In school, though, I was terrified to raise my hand. What if I was wrong? What if people looked at me?

When it came time to sell Girl Scout cookies, I was nervous. My parents wouldn't take my sales sheet to work. There was no Facebook at the time for social media selling. If I was going to sell the cookies, I was going to do it myself. The only way to do that was by knocking on doors. I practiced my sales pitch and set out, going door-to-door around the neighborhood. What turned me from speechless into a salesperson? A goal. When it came to selling cookies, I was focused on the prize, whether that was a T-shirt or a trip to Girl Scout camp. I'd scour the prize catalog with the same intensity reserved for my Scholastic book orders. I'd set a goal, and I'd pound the pavement to reach it.

Of course, I wanted to help my troop, too. I wanted us to be successful (and maybe win a pizza party, because in elementary school my dreams were simple). But that reward for doing my best, for putting myself out there, was the carrot on the stick. It motivated me to move on from rejection, and to hit "just one more house" even during the coldest Minnesota winter.

Now, decades later, I honestly can't remember the prizes I won. I still remember that feeling, though, of reaching my goal. It's a feeling I strive for today."

Tabitha Whissemore

It All Began
with a Bake Sale

One hundred years later, it's impossible to know which group of Girl Scouts first came up with the idea of selling cookies as a means to fund troop activities. Some say that the earliest sale was by Girl Scouts in Buffalo, New York; others point to stories about cookies sold by Illinois and Connecticut troops. These varied recollections about Girl Scout cookies' origins are understandable. Once the Girl Scout organization began in 1912, troops started springing up everywhere and each embraced the example set by the group's founder that girls should take matters into their own hands and make things happen.

The first *recorded* cookie sale in Girl Scout history took place in a small town in Oklahoma. Although no one is alive now who bought cookies at that historic Muskogee, Oklahoma, high school bake sale in 1917, the simple sugar cookies baked by the Mistletoe Troop, only months after they'd received their troop charter, are now listed on official Girl Scout documents as the start of the Girl Scouts selling cookies. This makes that historic bake sale the predecessor of one of the most successful entrepreneurial ventures in the United States.

When the girls from the Mistletoe Troop of Muskogee were deciding on the best way to raise money to buy supplies for their brothers and former male classmates stationed at Camp Bowie in Fort Worth, Texas, they had no idea that they would find such a prominent place in Girl Scout history. It was wartime, and all the girls had in mind was to raise enough money to send Christmas packages to hometown troops, most of whom would soon see action in the Great War (World War I). Those care packages included small necessities to lift the young soldiers' spirits and help them celebrate the holiday season with a few comforts from home—cigarettes, handkerchiefs, and makings for Christmas candy.

In December 1917, the girls made their famous cookies and sold them in the high school cafeteria. According to an article in the 1919 edition of the Girl Scout magazine, *The Rally*, the troop also made popcorn balls and sold them at basketball games. Had things turned out differently, we might now be celebrating Girl Scout popcorn balls. However, it was the cookie idea that resonated with their sister Scouts. *The Rally* article also includes a long report submitted by the troop on how the girls supported French war orphan Marie Louise Cottineau for two years, sold $104.46 worth of war stamps, and played Red Cross nurses in a "War Spectacular" at the Muskogee State Fair.

The Mistletoe Troop girls were as active in their war efforts as many troops are today in promoting respect and love of the environment. But the Oklahoma Girl Scouts' good deeds and works are not what they would be remembered for. It was their famed bake sale cookies that gave birth to the cookie program—the hallmark of self-sufficiency that remains the financial foundation of Girl Scouting.

In 1922, *The Rally*, once again, reported on cookie sales. This time it published a note from Miss Florence E. Neil, the local Girl Scout director in Chicago, Illinois. In this article, Neil described how Girl Scouts from all across Chicago had made a great deal of money selling cookies and, through the official Girl Scout magazine, she told the reading audience about their lessons learned. What she shared was a plan to mobilize the Scouts and build their treasuries through the sale of Girl Scout cookies.

For the Chicago sale, Neil said, girls made sugar cookies that cost about 30 cents for about eighty-four cookies. Next they packaged them by the dozen in wax paper bags and sold each bag for 25 to 30 cents, depending on their neighbors' ability to pay. Neil even included a recipe that the Chicago Girl Scouts had used, which was prefaced with the following challenge:

This is your chance to show how much Scouting means to you.

GIRL SCOUT COOKIES

- 1 cup of butter, or substitute
- 1 cup of sugar
- 2 tablespoons of milk
- 2 eggs
- 1 teaspoon of vanilla
- 2 cups of flour
- 2 teaspoons of baking powder

Cream butter and sugar, add well beaten eggs, then milk, flavoring, flour, and baking powder. Roll thin and bake in quick oven. (Sprinkle sugar on top.)

Stranger safety was as much on the minds of the Girl Scouts back in 1922 as it is today. Girls were told never to sell cookies in the street. "Sell them at school or to your neighbors or friends, or have a cookie sale in your neighborhood store."

In the spirit of friendly competition, an anonymous friend of the Girl Scouts, "who was greatly pleased at hearing that the Scouts are willing to help themselves by baking cookies," bought a silver loving cup award to give to the troop who sold the most cookies. The final incentive offered was a prize to the single Chicago Girl Scout who sold the most cookies. As a reward for her efforts, she was given one week at camp.

"If every Scout of the two thousand in Cook County bakes and sells one batch of cookies every month, the money taken in will amount to $2,000 a month," Neil calculated, "$24,000 for the entire year. Think it over. Is there *any* Scout who is not willing to do her share?" The article ended with these encouraging words:

"Attention Scouts! Forward! March! Bake! Sell!"

Cookie sales became widespread after Neil's story was published. As part of this national trend, Troop 6 of New Orleans, Louisiana, started their own cookie business. In a 1998 *New Orleans Magazine* interview with then-90-year-old Agnes Burke, she talked about baking cookies right in the heart of New Orleans. The silver-haired lady still had the treasured journal that she began as a twelve-year-old Scout that was filled with pictures and old stories clipped from the newspaper to remember her Girl Scouting experiences. In an article published during her troop's cookie sale, she was pictured with another Girl Scout at an American Legion Parade. In the photo, she was selling a bag of cookies to a veteran for 25 cents. That proud moment, captured in time, and her love of scouting stayed with her throughout her life.

While Agnes Burke fondly remembered her Girl Scout cookie days, another woman who claimed to have invented the concept of a "Girl Scout cookie," had less pleasant things to say. Bella Spewack, who worked as a public relations specialist for the Girl Scouts and Camp Fire Girls in the mid-20s, never spoke poorly of the Girl Scouts or their ideals, but she was reported to have said one very negative thing to say about the iconic cookies.

"I invented those heinous, heinous things—Girl Scout cookies," she is quoted as saying in Ruth Limmer's introduction to Spewack's memoir, *Streets*. Before the notion of branding was a familiar one, Spewack claimed to have come up with the idea of making the cookie sale more than just a simple sale. She thought that the cookies could become symbolic of the group's strong ideals. She also thought that cookie sales could be used to raise funds to support the National Organization.

As a young immigrant from Romania, Spewack's family lived in the lower east side of Manhattan. After high school graduation, she used her creative talents to get the word out to the media about the positive work of the Girl Scouts and Camp Fire Girls. Her *Los Angeles Times* 1990 obituary states that she came up with the idea of launching a national Girl Scout cookie sale while attending a flower show in New York. Seeing the girls in their uniforms make a lot of quick sales caused Spewack to make a creative connection. And although the national leadership didn't move on her ideas until many years later, she always felt that the creation of the cookie sale came from her inspiration. Spewack went on to work as a journalist and, with her husband, Samuel, wrote many plays. In 1948, they were asked to write the book for the Cole Porter musical, "Kiss Me Kate." Their work on that play won them two Tony Awards.

It's impossible to know why Spewack found the cookies to be so terrible, but in thinking about the socialite and theater crowd she became a part of as one of Cole Porter's entourage, it wouldn't be surprising if her quote about the cookies was born over cocktails in a scenario like this:

"You worked with those dreadful little Girl Scouts?"

"Oh yes, Darling. And it gets worse."

"Really? How could it be any worse than being around those campers in those ghastly green uniforms and dirty fingernails?

"Well, you'll probably never believe it but I invented those heinous, heinous, things—Girl Scout cookies."

"Those sugary little gut busters? For your penance, you naughty girl, the next party is at your place!"

Whether or not it happened just that way, Girl Scout cookie lovers still appreciate Spewack's inspired thinking, even if she did not. After Spewack's time working with the Girl Scouts, cookies sales, though not yet a national drive, continued to gain momentum through small local events.

In 1932, during the Great Depression, the Philadelphia Girl Scouts' cookie sale began with a baking demonstration. On an early November afternoon, from behind the windows of the Philadelphia Gas Works, a group of Scouts tempted all of those who passed by on foot, bicycle, or car with the delicious aroma of fresh baked cookies. The girls had originally planned just to show off their baking skills, but they were bombarded with requests from both the people who stopped to admire the plates of golden cookies and the gas company workers who were tantalized by the wafting smells. That day, most of the cookies went to the nearby child care center that had been promised the treats, but the entrepreneurs decided to sell the extras. The Philadelphia Scouts made a good profit from the day's work and used the money to support troop activities and to buy camping gear. By popular demand, they held another sale in 1933, which attracted a larger crowd and the media.

In 1934, the Philadelphia Girl Scouts contracted the Keebler Baking Company, which was based in Philadelphia at that time, to bake and package vanilla cookies in the shape of the Girl Scout symbol, the Trefoil. The baker agreed, and the first commercial cookies sale took place in Philadelphia in December of that year. Cookies sold for 23 cents a box or six boxes for $1.35. Reports of how successful the Philadelphia sale of packaged cookies reached the National Office.

In 1936, the first national Girl Scout cookie sale took place. Vanilla Trefoil cookies were shipped everywhere in the country—from Portland, Maine to Portland, Oregon. Legions of girls in green toted the boxes of cookies throughout their neighborhoods. The sale had two effects. The first was a large boost for the treasuries of each troop. With profits from the sale, they were able to do activities that would previously have taken them months, even years, to afford. The second outcome was that the words "Girl Scout Cookie" came to have meaning to Americans with and without daughters in the group. With this new national prominence, the Girl Scout organization became more popular and influential. In 1937, one hundred twenty-five councils nationwide decided to hold cookie sales.

The National Office felt that it was important to provide guidance to all councils about the best way to handle such a large sale, so they produced a brochure called *The Cookie Jar*. On the cover they wrote: "Such a sale, if wisely planned and well conducted, should result in a welcome addition to the income of the council and can be good Girl Scout publicity as well."

Within the booklet was advice on how to start a sale for those who were new to the process: (1) Read the procedures in *The Cookie Jar;* (2) Ensure against "inferior merchandise by patronizing a licensed baker; and (3) Write to the National Office for advice, if necessary.

At that time, cookie sales happened whenever the councils decided to hold them, so the book advised sellers to make the selling period brief: one to two days for smaller communities and a full week for larger cities and towns. During that time, girls were to pre-sell the cookies, with delivery a month or so later. The book also laid out tips about contracts, suggested the number and functions of adult volunteers needed to run a cookie sale, and gave pointers on how to keep track of the incoming funds. There was a strong warning to keep the girls safe during cookie sales, with the suggestion that they should use the buddy system when selling and take orders only from people they knew.

A supplement to *The Cookie Jar* soon followed, with an explanation to all of the local councils as to why the bakers had to pay royalties to the National Office for the license to make the classic Trefoil cookies. The royalty fees provided quality control over the cookies, allowed even the smallest council to participate in the sales, and offset the expenses that the National Office incurred in helping local councils sell cookies.

With the National Office's advice through *The Cookie Jar* and other useful materials, cookies sales grew each year, as did the size of the Girl Scout organization.

A few months before the 1939 New York cookie sale, the Greater New York Girl Scout Council decided to launch a slogan competition. Whoever came up with the cleverest way of expressing how good Girl Scout cookies were would win a sizable cash prize. To make certain that the judging was unbiased, the council enlisted the help of a committee of several creative wordsmiths—including Charles Hanson Townes, a critic, and Franklin P. Adams, the newspaper columnist—to choose the winner. Word about the competition was spread around by the Scouts at their activities. At Brooklyn's Memorial Presbyterian Church's dinner and fair, an unlikely person to win such a challenge heard about the contest from some Scouts and leaders working at a Girl Scout cookie booth.

Miss Annie B. Lyons was a longtime resident of Brooklyn and for the past six years she'd lived at the Graham Home for Old Ladies. The building, home to Lyons and eighty-nine other "old ladies," was owned by the Brooklyn Society for the Relief of Respectable Aged Indigent Females. The rules for living in the stately red brick dwelling were clear: Residents had to be at least sixty years old, live in Brooklyn or Williamsburg for at least the previous seven years, be recommended by at least one of the building's patrons, and, according to a 2001 article in the *Fort Greene Association Newsletter*, "bring satisfactory testimonials to the propriety of her conduct and respectability of her character." And although Lyons was up in age and had fallen on hard times, she still had a way with words.

When the judges read the entries, they were amused and impressed by Lyon's suggestion: Girl Scout cookies are *"The cookie that makes you scout for more."* According to the February 4, 1939, edition of the *New York Times*, for her witty use of a double entendre, Lyons received $150, which she accepted at the National Girl Scouts Headquarters on Lexington Avenue. Her slogan became the catchphrase for the 1939 New York cookie sale, and people from Manhattan to Staten Island had a chance to appreciate her clever phrasing when they spotted it on posters plastered throughout the city.

As the United States found itself drawn into World War II, cookie production slowed down. In 1942, only limited numbers of cookies were made because of what the Megowen-Educator Food Company, a licensed baker of the cookies, called "Pressures of government contracts plus the uncertain supply of raw materials, labor, and shipping." That year, the baker was able to give Scouts in New England a limited number of cookies to sell, but nothing close to meeting the demand for the product.

In 1944, the official Girl Scout newsletter offered good news about cookie supplies. "We are fortunate in being able to secure another resource for Girl Scout cookies. These cookies are of excellent quality...There will be a fair amount of stock available for shipment but at the present time shipments cannot be made to local councils west of the Rocky Mountains."

Although World War II was over in 1945, the end of the war did not mean that things became easier in organizing the national cookie sale. The continued sugar and shortening rationing made it impossible to manufacture cookies. Because so many councils and troops had come to depend on cookie sales to fund their programs, the National Office had to come up with an alternative product to sell. From 1944-1947, Girl Scouts sold official Girl Scout calendars, with, what an official publication called, "beautiful Scout-themed Kodachrome (color) photos." The National Office leadership suggested that any troops that were set on selling cookies should enlist the services of local bakeries. However, the bakers were strictly forbidden to use the Trefoil or any Girl Scout insignia on the cookies or boxes.

The recovery from World War II happened slowly, but by 1951, there were thirty-one licensed bakers who made the much-in-demand cookies, to the relief of the Scouts and anxious customers who had waited years to buy the tasty treats. In addition to the popular vanilla shortbread that had been around for so many years, there was also a sandwich cookie and a chocolate mint, an earlier version of Thin Mints. The real estate development of suburban homes that were built during this period, also affected how consumers got their cookies. In addition to door-to-door sales, cookies sales began at the new shopping mall.

As children from the post-war baby boom began going to kindergarten, and new schools were built to accommodate them, the number of girls who became Brownies, Juniors, Cadettes, and Senior Scouts also increased. Girl Scout cookies became a traditional treat that Americans in the cities, suburbs, and rural areas anticipated buying each year.

With each decade since the 50s, the types of Girl Scout cookies have increased, and the emotional attachment Girl Scouts and customers feel about the signature treats has grown. Whether purchased at a booth sale or a sale by a neighboring girl, for most, these cookies represent more than a dessert or snack. Girl Scout cookies allow us to support and respect the strengths of Girl Scouting, interact with neighbors, and give a nostalgic nod to our childhoods as we savor each crumb of a favorite American icon. ✌

"I was always really shy and never sold that many, but my family bought tons. And then the neighbors I sold to were rarely home to accept their orders and pay for them so we ended up with a freezer full of cookies, more than any family needs! And despite all those cookies, I was never near the top of the list of best sellers in my troop and never got any neat prizes. But I still love the cookies. Now with all the Girl Scout ice cream flavors and new cookie flavors…Ahhh!!!"

Jill Brodsky

Cookies by the Byte — From Doorbells to Digital Apps

From the earliest national Girl Scout cookie sale, American families looked forward to the knocks on their front doors that signaled the beginning of the cookie season. Girl Scouts of all ages came to sell their wares, armed with colorful order forms to tempt their neighbors with old favorites and new cookie flavors. Many people chose to split their orders among the influx of girls peddling the well-known cookies, as troop members in the last mid-century tended to live within blocks of one another.

Recently a friend told me that she used to buy so many cookies from neighborhood girls that they took up an entire freezer shelf, and she snacked on them all year long. However, it has been many years since a Girl Scout has come to her door, and she misses talking with and supporting Scouts without having to deal with the grocery store crowds at booth sales.

So how did the cookie sales strategy morph from being primarily a neighbor-to-neighbor enterprise to one that relies on booth sales and digital apps? To answer that question, it's helpful to use a long lens to see how the Girl Scouts changed as an organization from the turbulent 60s and 70s to the turn of the twenty-first century.

At the end of the 60s, the country was in the midst of a clash of generational views on large sweeping issues, such as the Vietnam War and civil rights, and also smaller but meaningful varying points of view on topics, such as fashion and music. In the late 60s, American girls transitioned from exclusively wearing dresses or skirts to school to sporting T-shirts with bell bottom jeans and other casual modes of dress in the classroom. Girl Scouts took notice of this shift and the option of wearing pants, which always had been worn for outdoor activities like camping, was allowed as part of the official uniform in the 70s. Reflecting the changing taste in music, Bob Dylan's "Blowing in the Wind" and other songs typically thought of as protest songs became staples sung around Girl Scout campfires across the nation.

At a time when the Civil Rights Act of 1968 gave Americans the hope that we were becoming a nation where people would be judged by their actions rather than by the color of their skin, the Girl Scouts were ahead of the curve. In fact, Martin Luther King described the Girl Scouts as "a force for desegregation" in 1956. The National Girl Scout organization has been a champion of civil rights and inclusion from its earliest days, with the first African American troop thought to be founded in 1924 in Tennessee by Josephine Groves Holloway.

According to the Girl Scouts of Middle Tennessee website and *Notable Black Women, Book 2,* Holloway, then recent Fisk University graduate, Josephine Groves, "became commissioned as a Girl Scout Captain" after having completed training given by Girl Scout founder Juliette Gordon Low. The trailblazer gave gold Girl Scout pins to as many as 300 young black women who "were brought into the registered platoon."

Unfortunately, when Holloway married just a few years later, she was forced to resign her position as a Girls Worker at the Bethlehem Center in Nashville because "a married woman would not have enough time for her work."

When she left her position, Holloway's Girl Scout commission also ended. And because her replacement at the center lacked interest in Girl Scouts, the first African American troop folded.

By the time Holloway was able to start another troop a few years later (between 1926-1933), the newly formed local Tennessee Girl Scout Council denied her a charter. Still believing in the Girl Scout ways, Holloway decided to lead an unofficial troop. Her girls wore alternative gingham garb instead of official uniforms, and they learned the Girl Scout laws and other doctrines from contraband manuals and handbooks that were purchased in Chicago by Holloway's husband, who was there for graduate school.

Those girls benefited from the Girl Scout teachings without the benefit of being official Scouts, but Holloway's troop was finally approved by the Tennessee council in 1943. As an official leader, Holloway continued her work with the Tennessee Girl Scout Council until her 1988 death at 90. In 1991, the Nashville Girl Scout Center honored her legacy by naming their historical and art collection in her memory.

In 1970 *The Milwaukee Journal* reported that the Girl Scouts held a Conference on Scouting for Black Girls in which long-range recommendations were made to "attract more adult minorities and try new media approaches." It was at this time that official handbooks began to include several images of Girl Scouts of color.

In 1975, as a sign of the organization's continuing commitment to diversity, Gloria Dean Randle Scott was selected to become the first African American National President of the Girl Scouts of America. According to the Girl Scouts website, "Her love of Girl Scouting blossomed through her involvement as a Girl Scout Junior in Troop 155, and in spite of the segregation her troop experienced, she learned unique leadership skills that would later propel her into her larger leadership roles. Scott served as the President of the Negro Girl Scout Senior Planning Board in the 1950s." She held the post of National President for three years (1975-78) and then went on to become the President of Bennett College in North Carolina.

One of the enduring changes that happened during Scott's national presidency was the creation of a Girl Scout pin designed to reflect the diversity of the Girl Scouts' membership. The modern-looking pin was based on a Saul Bass design. Bass, a graphic designer who won an Academy Award for his title sequences, created classic logos for several companies, including AT&T, Quaker Oats, and the Girl Scouts.

While reflecting on the new Girl Scout pin during a 2005 interview with NPR reporter Michele Martin, Scott said: "One of the ways that Girl Scouting nationally has made its commitment to pluralism…scouting for black girls and girls of other races…[was] that we ended up with a new pin. Our [new] Girl Scout pin is now 30 years old and it has the faces of girls and the three faces are ethnic faces out of bio-anthropology. And this is the whole notion of our commitment to pluralism."

Present day Girl Scouts can choose to wear either the modern pin described above by Scott, which is called the Official Girl Scout Membership Pin, or the gold trefoil pin, known as the Girl Scout Traditional Membership Pin. The many faces of Girl Scouts logo that is featured on the newer pin is also found on every Trefoil and Shortbread cookie.

Along with the diversification of the "face" of Girl Scouts, the 70s also brought into creation a new variety of cookie that was soon to become the second most popular flavor. In 1975, Samoas/Caramel deLites found their place on the cookie order form for the first time. A delightful combination of chocolate, caramel, and coconut on a vanilla cookie, more than 40 years later, the Samoa/ Caramel deLite is still a crowd favorite.

While the Girl Scout's famous fundraiser usually brings to mind the pleasure of eating cookies, in 1984 the National Girl Scout office was forced to block the sale of thousands of boxes of the product. In the first reported tampering scare of the beloved cookies, that year needles and paperclips were initially found in eight boxes of cookies in the St. Louis area. The FDA reported that it appeared that the objects had been pushed into the cardboard boxes. This event led to multiple copycat occurrences as *The Chicago Tribune* reported that "across the country, more than 850 cases of tampering were reported to federal authorities."

At the height of this scare, the Girl Scout's Executive Director Frances Hesselbein told the *New York Times*, "We have sold billions of cookies safely in this country for the past 48 years, and we are confident that the cookie sales will continue. I am confident that the American public is not going to permit anything like this to stop the cookie drive." However, this black mark on the cookies' reputation led to troops having to give refunds, thus cutting into their and the council's activities. In the end, the *Washington Post* reported that "sabotaged cookies were found in 18 states." St. Louis halted their cookie distribution with a third of their inventory still in warehouses.

The next year, all cookies were packaged in a new "tamper-free" box with a pull strip. In the 90s, perhaps in an effort to control such safety issues or perhaps just to give a sense of such standards, the National Girl Scout Office decided to limit the Girl Scout cookie bakeries to two—ABC Bakers and Little Brownie Bakers.

At the turn of the twenty-first century, 54 million of American households, or 51 percent, had at least one computer; according to the US Census Bureau, 44 million, or 42 percent, households had Internet access. In keeping with this new electronic world in which most children grew up with a computer mouse in hand, the Girl Scouts added badges and programs related to this new technology to all levels of their programs. With access increasing each year to faster information and communication, it was no surprise that the Girl Scout cookie sale was soon affected by the Internet.

In the winter of 2009, an eight-year-old Junior Scout named Wild Freeborn from Asheville, North Carolina, came up with an idea to help her reach her goal of selling 12,000 boxes of Girl Scout cookies—enough boxes to send her troop to summer camp. Her dad, Bryan, a professional Web designer, helped Wild publish a YouTube video in which she asked viewers to: "Buy cookies—they're yummy!" They also set up an online order system that was limited to customers within their local area (so Freeborn could personally deliver them). Her idea worked. She sold more than 700 boxes of cookies in record time. However, her innovative idea also got the National Girl Scout Office involved and vocal about Internet sales. By setting up a selling operation online, she violated Girl Scouts of the USA rules that ban Internet sales.

The Girl Scouts ordered Wild to take down her video and to stop selling cookies online. "The safety of our girls is always our chief concern," the Girl Scout national office wrote about the situation. "Girl Scout Cookie activities are designed to be face-to-face learning experiences for the girls." The Girl Scouts of the USA is very serious about all of Scouts' Internet interactions, and they have all Scouts and parents fill out a form that gives guidelines for Internet safety.

With the Girl Scouts' embrace of technology through their badges and patches, critics thought that the Scouts were missing a sales opportunity and were a little old fashioned with this take on technology. The Girl Scout's spokeswoman at the time, said, "Girl Scouts of the USA is not shunning the Internet ... though we still have to figure out how to do this." She went on to point out that online marketing of cookies was allowed, but actual sales were still forbidden.

As for Wild Freeborn, the whole cookie controversy got her and her father a trip to New York to appear on the *Today Show*, along with then Girl Scout Vice President of Public Relations, Denise Pesich. After hearing both sides of the controversy, host Matt Lauer asked Pesich, "Is it less safe to sell online than to go door to door in some communities?"

"When we sell door to door, we always have adults accompanying girls," Pesich replied. "In this case, we have a very concerned father overseeing the process, and we know she's relatively safe. But not in all cases is that true." She concluded that "the time will come when Girl Scouts can hawk their wares online—but that day isn't here yet."

In 2014, with the adoption of the Girl Scout's Digital Cookie™ computer application (www.girlscouts.org/en/cookies/all-about-cookies/digital-cookie.html), the day finally arrived when sanctioned cookie sales became possible through an Internet portal. This application was not meant to replace traditional Girl Scout cookie sales channels, such as door-to- door or booth sales, but "to help enhance in-person sales by allowing the girls to take orders more efficiently," Kelly Parisi, chief communications executive for the Girl Scouts of the USA told CNN.com.

The Digital Cookie platform provides girls with their current sales figures and lets them see what types of cookies are selling and where they may need to make changes. Depending on the affiliated council and the baker that the council uses, girls use either a personalized webpage or a digital application through which to make customer contact and sell cookies. On the website or app, customers can order cookies using credit cards. The key safety aspect of the Digital Cookie platform is that only those who are invited to buy cookies from individual Girl Scouts are allowed to access to those girls' stores.

Before they are allowed to create their own sales sites using the Digital Cookie app, Girl Scouts are must take the Digital Cookie pledge, which lays out guidelines for safe online interactions. Included among the three pages of pledge instructions (the following is a very abbreviated list from those instructions) are the following stipulations:

A GIRL SCOUT USING THE DIGITAL COOKIE PLATFORM MUST:

- review an Internet Safety pamphlet with her parents or guardians and get their permission to create her cookie sales website;
- sign only her first name to email messages;
- tell an adult right away if she comes across any information that makes her feel uncomfortable; and
- share the link to my Digital Cookie site with people that she knows in real life.

Also included is the promise that a girl will never set up an in-person meeting with someone she "meets" online through the Digital Cookie site, other than to deliver cookies to customers approved (and usually accompanied) by parents or guardians. The final pledge requirements pertain to basic long-held Girl Scout cookie sales safety rules—use the buddy system, never deliver cookies after dark, and never enter a customer's home.

For those who do not receive invitations to online cookie stores, there are online cookie locators and an app called the Girl Scout Cookie Finder that lets potential cookie customers know where the nearest booth sales are being held. These electronic cookie compasses are only useful for a few months each year, usually in March for councils with spring sales and in October and November for the one council with a fall sale.

While it may seem that Girl Scouts are less visible than in the past, the changing times have brought new means to purchase cookies. Councils and the troops appreciate all purchases because the cookie program is as valuable as ever to Girl Scouts (and the cookies are just as delicious). So the next time you bite into a Thin Mint or another favorite Girl Scout cookie, keep in mind all of the opportunities that will be afforded to twenty-first-century Girl Scouts, thanks to the skills they gain from participating in the cookie program. ❧

"My mom was the cookie mother when I was a Brownie. Our entire basement was filled with boxes upon boxes of cookies. It felt like Willy Wonka's Chocolate Factory emerged overnight in my house. A little path led from the basement door to a 4x4 space in front of the TV. The rest was a cardboard oasis of Samoas, Trefoils, Tagalongs, Do-Si-Dos, and, of course, Thin Mints. My brother and I tore right in to the boxes, under the false pretense that our mom had purchased us a lifetime supply of Girl Scout cookies. Now, my mom is a meticulous type of person, so all of the cookies were organized into piles for each Scout. Alas, the cookies were not ours, but the consequences were."

Robyn Barberry

PART TWO

Council Perspective

Not Your Mother's Cookie Sale

S omething caught me by surprise when I walked through the doors of the Washington, DC, Girl Scouts Headquarters. I had carefully selected a sage green pantsuit to wear on my fact-finding mission to learn about the cookie sales operation at the Girl Scout Council of the Nation's Capital (GSCNC). I'd pictured their Headquarters as a scene that could rival the Pentagon for its array of uniforms, so clad in green, I'd be sure to fit right in. I pushed open the glass door to the mezzanine business suite early one October morning and found myself to be the only one wearing green—there wasn't a uniformed staff member in sight. This was not my mother's Girl Scouts experience. It wasn't even the Girl Scouts of my youth. This sleek office filled with casually clothed employees was a nerve center of twenty-first-century Girl Scouting.

Standing next to the receptionist's desk was an attractive blonde woman holding a clipboard. "Julie?" I asked as I approached the desk. Indeed, I had found my guide to the world of Girl Scouts and their iconic cookies. Julie Carlson, the Product Sales Manager who handles all of the cookie sales for this council had kindly agreed to tell me about her job as the head cookie honcho for the DC area. She asked me to sign the guest log and handed me a visitor's badge to wear. I clipped on the plastic credentials and followed her down the corridor.

"We don't have private offices," she said, "so I think the best place to talk is in here." She pointed toward a small meeting space—a cubicle furnished with a small round table and two chairs. "We call this a pod," she said as I followed her in and sat down across from her. Her shoulder-length hair was pulled into a loose ponytail and a sprinkling of freckles sat on her tanned cheeks. She was wearing a short-sleeved white blouse and black cotton slacks. With her athletic build and high energy level so early in the morning, I could easily picture her putting on a fully loaded backpack and leading me on a five-mile hike. Her breezy manner instantly put me at ease.

I was curious as to what led Julie to the path of working with Girl Scouts in general and cookies sales in particular, so we started our interview there. She'd been a Girl Scout through twelfth grade. "I must say most people didn't know that. Even in the late 60s, being a Scout was kind of a covert activity."

She started her professional career as a visual merchandiser in the late 70s for Woodward and Lothrop, a favorite Washington, DC, department store of years gone by, designing in-store displays and managing the customer service departments. She worked for 22 years in various stores until the retail chain went out of business. Next, after spending three years at home, she started volunteering for the Girl Scouts, first as a service unit manager and then as a leader trainer.

Her career with GSCNC advanced quickly. "When an opportunity arose to work as a field director, I took that job. That was in August 1999 and so I worked for eight years as a field director, recruiting leaders and that kind of stuff, and then in February 2007, I made the jump to product sales. I was looking at a position that had council-wide impact, and this position certainly does."

Thinking back about herself as a young Scout, Julie remembers being a motivated cookie sales person as she grew up in Prince Georges County, Maryland. She was one of five kids in her family, and all of the girls were Scouts. "We went for blocks and blocks going door to door with our wagons selling cookies," she recalled. "And I do remember quite clearly standing outside of the Giant (Supermarket) for booth sales. It was March and we were shivering as we sold boxes of cookies."

When asked if she thought her early entrepreneurial training as a scout helped her in her retail career and her work overseeing cookie sales, she thought for a moment before she said, "I sort of fell into retail, but it came pretty naturally. So I don't know… it's possible. I never really thought about that connection." Now she is the mother of four girls, and all of her daughters have been Girl Scouts."

Girl Scout cookies are baked by two suppliers—Little Brownie Bakers (a subsidiary of Kellogg) in Lexington, Kentucky, and ABC/Interbake in Richmond, Virginia. Both bakeries have been in the Girl Scout cookie baking biz for years—Little Brownie since 1975 and ABC Bakers, one of the first to manufacture the treats, since 1939.

Both bakeries make the five varieties of cookies that all customers have come to know and love, but for the most part, they brand similar cookies with different names. What Little Brownie calls a *Samoa* cookie, ABC calls *Caramel deLites*. ABC's *Peanut Butter Sandwich* cookies are called *Do-Si-Dos* by Little Brownie. Little Brownie's *Tagalong* cookies—a chocolate-covered peanut butter patty on a vanilla cookie—are ABC's *Peanut Butter Patties*. The counterpart to the vanilla Trefoil-shaped *Shortbread* cookies made by ABC are called *Trefoils* by Little Brownie. The top selling *Thin Mint* does not suffer from this identity crisis. Both companies call it by the same name. (See a side by side comparison on page 170.)

In addition to those five favorite cookie types, both bakeries rotate new flavors in and out just to keep things interesting. Sometimes the new options aren't terribly popular. During the sales period a few years ago, Little Brownie Bakers introduced the Little Brownie cookie, which was sugar-free. In the middle of March, when troops brought in their slow-selling cookies to exchange them for popular sellers like Thin Mints, the DC council ended up with about 400 cases of the sugar-free Little Brownie cookies. "We ended up offering them to the veterans' home in Southern Maryland, and they said they would love to have them because they have such a high number of diabetic residents...so they took 100 cases. Buoyed by that, we started calling nursing homes and found a place for every cookie."

The Little Brownie cookie has been retired but since then there have been other sugar-free options, including a chocolate chip cookie, simply called Sugar Free Chocolate Chips. "That one," Julie assured me, "was very tasty."

Both bakeries offer new options annually, but customers in the DC area will only be aware of what is offered by Little Brownie. Julie thinks that competition between the suppliers is a good thing, and she tells me that many years ago there were more than 20 cookie manufacturers during a single sales season. Each Girl Scout council chooses the bakery that they want to buy from. Of the 112 councils throughout the United States, about 60 percent of them decided to go with Little Brownie and the others with ABC.

"Competition is important in any industry because each individual council chooses which baker to buy from," Julie tells me. "And as long as there is competition, there is innovation because each baker needs to make their package attractive to the council and to customers."

"So do you get samples?" I asked, with thoughts of suggesting a coffee break with cookies.

"We certainly do. We get cookies from the bakery that are strictly for public relations. We use them quite a bit in the fund development field, as we're looking for grants. Because cookies are so tightly entrenched in the Girl Scout image that wherever you go, you HAVE to have cookies. Maybe it's my retail background, but those cookies are assets and we don't just give them away."

GSCNC hasn't held a cookie-to-cookie taste test between the two companies' products for some time, but Julie reported that the competition between Little Brownie and ABC in the past decade has heated up. "When I was a new product representative, both bakeries aggressively sought my attention." At that time, less than a decade ago, both bakers courted councils nationwide because the Girl Scouts of the USA was going through a "realignment." This reorganization brought together several very small councils. "Some of the councils were smaller than Southern Maryland, which is part of the DC council." To correct this situation, the Girl Scouts' National Office made the move toward "high capacity" councils, like GSCNC whose membership is currently about 57,000 girls in approximately 5,000 troops.

"One example of a group of councils in need of realignment was in the Los Angeles area, where they had five councils that were all competing for the same resources, the same marketing, the same media." Another realigned council, The Heart of Pennsylvania Council, was the product of a merger of four or five small councils. GSCNC was also affected by the realignment, Julie explained. "We picked up Winchester and Culpepper, Virginia, and other regions in the same area that are currently in the West Virginia council. The idea was to bring together all of the regions in the DC area, so soon now we'll have suburban, urban, and rural troops. We may be the largest council in the nation."

So what does all of this realignment business have to do with cookie sales? According to Julie, Little Brownie and ABC had to present themselves again to all of these realigned councils. "I think the realignments inspired manufacturers to make their program materials really top notch. I know that in Pennsylvania, three of the realigned councils had used ABC Bakeries and one used Little Brownie, and the new council went with Little Brownie. I don't remember which group ended up as the big winner. Personally, I think that Little Brownie's Thin Mint is better, flavor wise."

Julie's preference for Little Brownie's cookies is a long held opinion at GSCNC—Little Brownie has been the manufacturer of choice for this council for over thirty years. And that choice has yielded record sales: the net cookie sale for the DC Council is $17.1 million. "We, as a council, have achieved top sales for the past six years running in the country," Julie said proudly. "We are not the largest council geographically, and we don't have the largest girl membership. I don't know what that says about the DC area but either they are really good supporters or they really love cookies."

Each year, GSCNC holds what is called a "spring sale," one that starts in January when Scouts take the initial orders. "In February, the deliveries start coming from the bakery, and they are delivered throughout the council through George Washington's Birthday. Ideally by the third week of February, the Scouts have delivered cookies to everyone who ordered them. Then March is our booth sales time—the direct sales portion of the campaign. Cookie sales is a three-month process."

The Girl Scouts of Central Maryland (a neighboring council to GSCNC) is the last council to hold a fall sale. Julie has her misgivings about the timing of such a sale.

"Right off the bat, coming off of the summer break, you must have troops organized, ready to do their sales. Sometimes that is a challenge. To maximize the sales and the ability of troops to participate, I think that the spring sales work best."

Each council sets the price for a box of cookies and GSCNC has set their price at $4 a box, with a couple of specialty cookies, including a gluten free option, selling for $5. But there are places in the country where every box of cookies sells for $5. "And it's really based on the council's needs." Julie said. "Without a doubt, the cookie sale drives the budget. The money we make on cookie sales is about sixty to seventy percent of our budget. The troops get 65 cents per box sold. All troops can get up to 75 cents if their sales figure is high enough and they forego the incentives. At that point in their lives, most teen girls have had all of the stuff that we offer as incentives. They want to go on trips, so they really need the cash." Last year the GSCNC troops added more than $2.96 million to their treasuries from selling 4.2 million boxes of cookies.

I want to know more about the incentives, so Julie fills me in. "Incentives are always program based, and this year our theme is 'Built by Girls' to commemorate 100 years of Girl Scouts selling cookies."

Beyond the tangible benefits of participating in the cookie sales—incentives and money for the troop treasury—there are also less concrete rewards. Julie stressed that the cookie sales itself is program driven. "It isn't just about making money. A troop can easily make $800 without really trying. But my point has always been that to make $800 and have no goals as to what you're doing with it is not half as successful as when the girls decide what they need or what they want to do with the proceeds and then set troop and individual goals and try to meet them."

The program materials that the cookie manufacturers produce on behalf of the Girl Scouts include strong goal-setting components. Even the order cards have a place on them for girls to write down their individual goals and to remind them of the troop goals. Ideally, troops should decide as a group what to do with the proceeds of their sales efforts. Julie explained how she handled this when she was a troop leader. "I'd ask them 'What do we want to do this year? What kind of activities do we need to fund?' The girls inevitably said 'We want to go to Disneyworld.' So we'd start with that. I said, 'Okay, it's going to cost the troop a total of $2,500 for each girl to go and we make 65 cents per box. So this is how many boxes of cookies that we need to sell.' Then the girls became more realistic and asked, 'Can we go to the zoo?' So it's a learning process for the girls to understand what they can afford. And I urge leaders to go through that process because a lot of troops just do stuff in the fall and say, 'The cookies will pay us back later.' But then it just teaches girls to use credit, for heaven's sake. So let's not do that. Let's let them decide what they want to do—even the youngest girls—based on the cost of the activity and let them set their goals based on that."

In thinking about and comparing how cookie sales have changed since the time she was a girl to now when she is leading the charge in the twenty-first century, Julie offered that GSCNC has looked at this quite a bit recently. Despite the successful $17.1 million that the council raised in its 2015 cookie sale, "we have had a flat trend for several years that is compounded by the fact that our membership is also flat. It's not growing as much as in the past simply because girls have so much to choose from these days—select sports and everything else. When I was a girl, you were either a Girl Scout or a Campfire Girl. That's what you did. So there are just so many more options now. I think that the parents' personal concern for safety has inhibited door-to-door sales. I get calls all of the time from potential customers who ask me 'Are you selling cookies? Nobody came to my door.'

"We do have guidelines that we ask girls to follow: that they only sell during daylight hours and that parents are supervising. So when you have a parent who may be commuting an hour and a half each way, and they get home at seven o'clock, it's hard for them to get excited about cookie sales because it's dark because it's January. And parents are rightly so more protective. I remember going blocks from home with my little wagon and money. I always had a buddy with me, but it wasn't always an adult. Parents are a lot more concerned about their girls being out. I think that booth sales are probably a greater percentage of our sales now." The GSCNC hasn't yet signed up to participate in the new Digital Cookie sales platform but that may happen in the next year or two.

When asked if any troops decide against participating in the cookie sales, Julie sighed heavily and said that there are a few. When she asked the holdouts why they chose not to participate, the response was generally that the parents don't want to be bothered. "So I say to them, 'You do realize that the sales support council? That it isn't just for the troop participation? It's a service project to keep this council running and operational.' I'm not saying it's not hard work, but there are certainly benefits to it. We certainly urge and recommend that troops do participate but it is a voluntary operation."

On the other side of that coin, several troops in GSCNC are "super sellers." Those girls and their leaders are always looking for new ways to market and reach out to people. One such teen troop approached real estate agents and said, "You can buy cookies for baskets for each house that you sell and we'll make it pretty and wrap it and deliver it to you or to the house, however you want it." That group of girls got quite a few sales out from that pitch. Other enterprising troops have approached hotels to see if they could put it in each guest room in the month of March.

Some of these ideas are inspired by the program materials created by the cookie manufacturers who put colorful creative material online for Girl Scouts to download. "Little Brownies have done a lot for the teens. They have put together a web-based program so girls can go online to get business card templates, and they can get PowerPoint presentations that they can make to businesses. The push is to get these girls to look at the cookie sale as if it were their own business. And to take it a step further, they learn to make professional presentations."

How does GSCNC recognize these top-selling troops? Any girl who sells 500 boxes or more receives a certificate of honor from the council, and they get a letter of congratulations from the Assistant Executive Director. Julie explained that "there are councils that do very big events, shout girls' names from the roof tops. We have a little different philosophy—and it does come from the top down—that all effort is appreciated, and that the girl who has a 1,000-box sale probably also has very strong parental support to sell an extraordinary amount of cookies. And her effort is no more appreciated than the girl who has little to no parental support and sells 50 boxes of cookies totally on her own and makes all of the deliveries."

As a final point, Julie told me what she hopes that each Girl Scout will gain from participating in the cookie sale. "They really should get that whole teamwork, goal setting, financial management, and thinking of those things at each step along the way. I don't think that every troop gets that experience. And the whole sales process teaches life skills. You know when I tell people that, sometimes they kind of roll their eyes at me and say 'Yeah, okay' but it seriously does."

"I had amazing troop leaders. I was in the same troop from the time that I was a Brownie until eighth grade. They were like moms. We couldn't get away with anything with them. And it wasn't until I was a troop leader that I asked myself, 'How did they do what they did?' In my memory we camped all of the time. We probably camped twice a season but to me, we were going every other weekend. So one year I sent notes to both of the women saying, 'I'm a Girl Scout leader now and how you guys did this I will never know.'"

"Because I still remember things that they said and I find myself saying things that they said. I really believe that the relationship of the troop leader with the girl is a relationship they don't have with any other adult. She's not a teacher, she's not a mom, she's not a friend, but she's an older confidante, somebody who can help. I think it's important. I loved having that and every now and then I'll run into one of the girls from the troop I led who's now in college, she'll say, 'I was in your Girl Scout troop!'"

In just one hour, Julie had filled me in on the day-to-day business of selling Girl Scout cookies in a way that only one who eats, sleeps, and breathes cookies could. Still I had to ask her the one inevitable question that she's come to expect.

"What's your favorite Girl Scout cookie?" I asked as I gathered my things to go.

"Tagalongs, without a doubt," Julie says quickly. "I like the Thin Mint, of course, and the Trefoil is perfect with coffee. But Tagalongs would get the prize, without even blinking an eye." ❧

"In 2015 there was a cookie shortage in our council and my troop ran out of cookies. Consequently, we couldn't get more to do booth sales. A first-year Junior from another troop, Daphne W., heard about our predicament, and she offered to do a booth with my daughter. We weren't in the same service unit or troop, but she offered to bring all the cookies she had and whatever the two girls sold at the booth she would give my daughter her half of the sales money and transfer the correlating number of cookies. Now mind you there was no guarantee she would ever get more cookies and the most troops could hope get after the announcement was an additional five cases. Had Daphne not shared with my daughter Allison, who was a Brownie at the time, she would have never exceeded her goal or be honored as a top cookie seller in our service unit. Daphne was and is a true sister Scout. We were lucky that events in her troop brought her to join our troop. In 2016 Daphne helped Daisy and Brownies from various troops with less experience learn the ropes of door-to-door cookie sales. She also blew away her goal of 1500 boxes and sold 1800 boxes. My best estimate is that had she sold solo she would have hit the 3000+ mark, but she loves helping others and being with her fellow Scouts."

Dede Neufeld

Welcome to Cookie College

Battle Hymn of the Cookie Sale
(To the tune of "The Battle Hymn of the Republic")

We're selling Girl Scout cookies,
Yes, it's Girl Scout Cookie time!
"Would you like to buy some?"
Is our cookie-selling line.
We've got lots to choose from,
Don't you see your favorite kind?
We thank you very much!

Glory, glory, we are Girl Scouts!
Smiling, cookie-selling Girl Scouts!
Please buy cookies, you can help us.
We can't eat them all ourselves!

That February afternoon was all about the cookies. As Girl Scout staff members and other volunteers got ready by putting construction paper into neat piles, straightening posters, and thumbing through registration materials, in the distance was the tap, tap, tap of small feet running down the stairs and through the hallways. Outside the temperatures in Chevy Chase, Maryland, were near freezing and a thin layer of ice slowed the long line of minivans and SUVs creeping down a long driveway. Once inside the Four-H Conference Center, Girl Scouts from the

District of Columbia, Maryland, and Virginia flung their coats and scarves into the arms of their leaders and mothers. Free from their pastel-colored Lands End parkas, puffy down-filled coats, and dark North Face jackets, the younger Scouts in brown vests and their older sister Scouts in green giggled, jumped, and then rushed in bunches to the long registration table to sign into Cookie College. Troop members were all assigned to the same activity group but they had the chance to make new friends with the girls from all over that area who were also assigned to that group. Most of the girls didn't know what to expect, but they were all excited to learn more about the best ways to sell Girl Scout cookies.

On the other side of the registration table, Cookie Professors—women who ranged from teens to silver-haired volunteers—checked the girls in by troop number. These instructors who'd made time on a Saturday afternoon to help girls improve their selling skills were a rainbow of African American, white, Hispanic, and Asian women, all dressed to move in comfortable clothes and sneakers. Some of the Cookie Professors were professionals from the local Girl Scout office, joined by Girl Scout volunteers. Others were friends of Girl Scouting from the DC metro community who held a variety of jobs—college students, bankers, members of the media, and stay-at-home moms. Whether young or old, working inside the home or out, what all of these women had in common was that they loved Girl Scout cookies and that they understood the importance of the cookie program to today's Girl Scouts.

❧

When most people think of Girl Scout cookie time, they think of the cookies themselves—the excitement of eating the first Thin Mint or Samoa of the season—or the act of supporting Girl Scouts by buying cookies. However, there's another equally important aspect of the annual sale. Most women who grew up as Girl Scouts say that the skills that girls acquire as they sell cookies are ones that laid the foundation for many aspects of their future success. According to the Girl Scouts of the USA, the five essential skills that the Cookie Program helps participating girls to develop are:

1. **Goal Setting**: Girls set cookie sales goals and, with their team, create a plan to reach them. This matters because girls need to know how to set and reach goals to succeed in school, on the job, and in life.
2. **Decision Making**: Girls decide where and when to sell cookies, how to market their sale, and what to do with their earnings. This matters because girls must make many decisions, big and small, in their lives. Learning this skill helps them make good ones.
3. **Money Management**: Girls develop a budget, take cookie orders, and handle customers' money. This matters because girls need to know how to handle money—from their lunch money to their allowance to (someday) their paycheck.
4. **People Skills**: Girls learn how to talk (and listen!) to their customers, as well as learning how to work as a team with other girls. This matters because it helps them do better in school (on group projects, on sports teams, and on the playground) and, later, at work.
5. **Business Ethics**: Girls act honestly and responsibly during every step of the cookie sale. This matters because employers want to hire ethical employees—and the world needs ethical leaders in every field.

The goal of the DC Cookie College and similar events (e.g., Cookie Rally or Nutty University) held by councils across the United States, was to help reinforce these skills and knowledge in the Brownie and Junior Scouts who've come to participate in the day's activities.

᠐

"If you are a Samoa, line up behind me," a young woman said to the auditorium of Girl Scouts. Homeroom—a short welcome speech by a Girl Scout council staff member and a brief explanation of how the afternoon would be spent—was over, and it was time for the Girl Scouts to move into the next part of the day's agenda. A combination of Brownie and Junior Scouts filed through the rows of chairs to get in place so that they could go to their first "class" of the day. The other groups, the Thin Mints, Do-Si-Dos, Tag Alongs, and Trefoils—each group named after a particular Girl Scout cookie—also lined up to go to classrooms where cookie-related activities were to be held. For the next two hours, each girl would attend half-hour classes in art, drama, music, and "Money Matters." And, upon completion of the cookie curriculum, more than 100 girls would return to the auditorium for graduation.

The auditorium was the site of the music class, so the Samoa group sat in the first few rows of the large room. Julie Carlson, the Girl Scout Council of the Nation's Capital cookie program sales manager, stood in front of the girls.

"Does anybody here know the song 'Are You Sleeping?'" Most of the Scouts raised their hands as Julie's helpers—other professors—passed out song lyrics to the group.

"Well, today we're going to use that tune to sing another song about Girl Scout cookies. If you look on your paper, you'll see the song 'Yum Yum Yum.' Let's give it a try now." After giving them a chance to scan the lyrics Julie started singing and the girls quickly joined in.

Girl Scout Cookies, Girl Scout Cookies,
Yum, Yum, Yum; Yum, Yum, Yum
Eat 'em by the dozen, Eat 'em by the dozen
They're all gone, They're all gone.

Once the Girl Scouts mastered the first song, they enthusiastically sang "Buy Some Cookies" (sung to the tune of "Pop Goes the Weasel") and "Girl Scout Cookies" (sung to the tune of "Jingle Bells").

Girl Scout Cookies, Girl Scout Cookies
Shortbreads are the best…

The half hour went by quickly, and it was time for this group to move on to art class as the next group of Scouts galloped to the front of the auditorium to have their turn singing about cookies.

After taking a twist and a turn through the halls of the conference center, the Samoas entered one of the classrooms and sat down on stools. On the tables in front of them were colorful markers, poster paint, glitter, glue, and poster board. The art professor instructed her new students to don smocks—men's shirts donated just for this purpose—to protect their uniforms. The girls rushed over to a pile of large long-sleeve shirts to pick one out. With some effort, they got them buttoned and then waited for the next instructions.

"Who's seen posters for different events in their church or recreation centers?" a young professor with a long dark ponytail asked. A few hands went up. "Today we're going to make posters so you can advertise Girl Scout cookies."

One of the girls timidly raised her hand. "What if you don't go to church?"

"That's okay. You can put the poster up anywhere. At school or at the grocery store. You have to ask an adult if it's okay though. The other thing is that you can't put your name or phone number on the poster. Does anyone have an idea why you wouldn't put your phone number on the poster?"

"Because you might not be home?"

"Because you don't want to get a lot of calls on your cell?"

"Because you might not be safe if you put your name and number on the poster?"

"That's right. We want to be safe sellers. And anyway, the posters are just to remind people that it's Girl Scout cookie time. Who's ready to get started on their poster?"

Some of the girls carefully sketched out their ideas and others grabbed a brush and glopped on paint. Markers squeaked as some of the group's creations were completed, and others added layers of glitter and glue for finishing touches. At the end of twenty minutes, the girls presented their posters to one another. *Buy Girl Scout Cookies* was the most popular headline, but the artwork was as diverse and unique as the girls who created it.

"You can pick up your posters at the end of the day, so that they have the chance to dry," the art professor told the group as they headed off to the next session. It was time for drama class.

The Samoas sat down on the floor cross legged as their drama professor organized a box of props. She welcomed the girls to her class and asked for three volunteers.

"One of you will be the customer and two of you will be the Girl Scouts selling cookies. Who can tell me why we need two Scouts?"

"You have to sell with a buddy for safety," one of the girls volunteered.

"Right! So you," she pointed to a Junior Scout, "are the customer. And you two," she pointed to two Brownies, "are selling cookies. Before they get started, who has any ideas about what to say to people to make them want to buy cookies? We call those sales pitches." She pointed to a Brownie in the front row who had an idea.

"That the cookies are fresh and delicious?" The instructor nodded her head and pointed to another girl.

"I say that the cookies are only around for a short time so you'd better buy them before it's too late."

"I say that the cookies help our troop get to do activities," a Junior Scout added.

"Great! Those are all good ideas. Now that we've heard some ideas from the group, it's time for our selling skit. Let's see if you girls," she points to the Brownies, "can sell our customer some cookies. Use your best sales pitch."

The girls pretended to ring a doorbell and then attempted to convince their Junior Scout "customer," to buy some cookies. The customer, a tough sell, had several objections to which the younger girls didn't know how to respond. Finally, the Junior Scout gave in and bought one box of cookies.

"That's great. Let's give our actors a round of applause." The group clapped politely and the young actors sat down. "Who knows anything about using the Internet to help you sell cookies?" None of the girls' hands went up. One of the leaders who's been following her girls from room to room and sitting quietly in the back raised her hand.

"Are we allowed to sell on the Internet?" she asks. "I always thought that you couldn't do that."

"You are absolutely right," the drama professor said to the concerned leader. "In our council, Girl Scouts are not allowed to directly sell cookies on the Internet. But we are allowed to send emails to people asking them if they'd like to buy cookies from you. That's perfectly okay. The main thing is to only send emails people you know. Should we do a skit about emailing friends now?" After nods of affirmation, two girls acted out a scene where one sent an email and the other received it. After a few more scenarios, it was time to move on to the Money Matters class.

"Don't forget," the drama professor said as she sent the Samoas on their way, "Always sell with a buddy, don't send emails to strangers, and let people know how much you learn from selling cookies!"

When the Samoas arrived at the Money Matters class, the professors were counting out dollar bills and putting coins into neat stacks in the center of the tables. Also at each seat was a small pad and sharpened yellow pencil.

One of the Samoas looked upset. "This isn't a math class, is it? I hate math," she muttered.

"Welcome," said a young woman in wire-frame glasses, "We're here to learn about managing your money. Who here gets an allowance?" Several of the girls raised their hands. "Great! Well we're going to talk about your troop's money—the money you make from selling cookies."

She pointed to a poster on the wall that listed a dozen activities that Girl Scouts have participated in. "When you sell cookies, you can do a lot of neat things with the money like camping, going to the aquarium, taking a trip to the Juliette Gordon Low Birthplace in Savannah, or even going to Disney World. Those activities listed are just a few of the ideas that we came up with. Does anyone know how much money your troop gets when you sell a box of cookies?" A few girls had guesses that were close, but only one comes up with the correct figure—65 cents.

"So if your troop was going to go camping, and it costs 65 dollars to go, how many boxes of cookies would your troop have to sell?" The girls picked up their pencils to solve the problem.

One girl raised her hand. "Do we have a calculator?"

"You don't need a calculator for this one," the professor responded. "This isn't school. You all can help each other." The girl talked across the table and finally, they came up with the right number.

"100 boxes!" a Junior Scout shouted.

"Good. So let's say, you wanted to go to Disney World. And let's guess that it costs $650 each for every girl to go. How many boxes would every girl in your troop have to sell to get there?"

"A whole lot!" a Brownie said. The group laughed.

"1,000 boxes," another girl offered.

"That's right." The Money Matters professor surveyed around the room. "Does anyone want to share what your troop has decided to do with your cookie money?"

"We're going to Kings Dominion!"

"We're going bowling!"

"We're going to buy troop T-shirts so we won't get lost on field trips!"

"Wow! Those are all great goals. To get you ready for booth sales, we're going to practice selling cookies and making change for customers. You all know that a box of cookies sells for 4 dollars, right? How much change do you give someone if they buy one box of cookies and give you a 5-dollar bill?"

"A dollar?"

"Right. So, in the middle of your table is pretend money. I want everybody take turns buying cookies from the person next to you and making change." The girls scoop up the money and practice doling out the bills and plastic coins, with some help from the adult volunteers and their leaders.

"We're almost done," the woman said, calling the group back to order. "Can anyone tell me what you might do if you realize that someone has forgotten their change on your cookie booth table?"

"Run to catch them and give it back?"

"That's a good idea. What if you don't see them?" No one has an idea, so she continues. "If you can't find them, maybe you could buy a box of cookies with the money for your Gift of Caring charity." The girls nodded. "What happens if you accidentally lose money while you're delivering cookies?"

"Tell your mom or leader?" one Scout answered shyly.

"That's right. Always tell an adult when there is a problem. Well, it looks like you girls are ready for graduation from Cookie College!" The girls gathered their belongings to leave the classroom. "Good luck on your cookie sales," the Money Matters professor called after them as they walked back toward the auditorium.

Once all of the groups took their seats, one of the Cookie Professors takes the stage. The girls were squirming in their seats with anticipation.

"Congratulations!" The Girl Scout staffer spoke into a microphone so that she could be heard over the excited chatting of her audience. "You've completed Cookie College, and it's time for graduation. You girls should be very proud of yourselves. Today you've learned about the best ways to sell your cookies, staying safe while selling, and the best way to handle money during the cookie sale. You can even sing about cookies! Who's going to use what they learned here to sell more cookies?"

Almost all of the girls waved their hands in the air. "Fantastic! So that you all have the chance to walk across the stage, I'm going to call you up by groups. You'll get your patches and certificate from your leaders, but we want to congratulate you right now in person. The first group to come up here is: The Thin Mints!"

A clump of Scouts rose and walked down the aisle to the stage steps. They proudly marched across the stage; a few girls raised their arms in victory and one took a bow. After a few more groups were called up, the Samoas finally had their turn. The girls in the audience clapped as the Juniors and Brownies in this group skipped and ran from one side of the stage to the other.

As the girls put on their coats to leave, one young Scout turned to her leader with a request. "Can we stop for a snack on the way home?" she asked. "All of this talk about cookies has made me hungry!" ❧

"I enjoyed being a Girl Scout when I was growing up, so I encouraged my three daughters to join the Scouts. And they did. When Girl Scout cookie sales seasons came around, I was ready to do my part by selling to my coworkers. One year, a week before the official start of the sale, one of my colleagues posted her cookie order form in the lunch room. I had just been to a workshop where they stressed the importance of honoring the start date, so I was annoyed but even more so because a bunch of people were signing up to buy them! I'm pretty sure I asked the HR guy to take her order sheet down, but I don't think he did. It just goes to show how parents sometime get into the sales as much as (or more than) their daughters."

Patricia Marshall

PART THREE

Troop Perspective

From Girl Drama to Girl Power — Meet Troop 2288

Now that you have some historical background on the Girl Scout cookie sale and a sense of how those sales work on the Council level, let's take a look at the girls in modern-day Girl Scout troops and the women who lead them. The following chapters are my observations from shadowing one troop during the 2008 cookie sales season. Though a few years have passed since that time, the basics of troops' cookie sales experiences remain the same.

When you meet Jennifer M. for the first time, it's hard to imagine her physically being able to keep up with a troop of rambunctious preteen and teen Girl Scouts because of her halting walk that comes from constant knee pain. At work and at play, she favors colorful oversized shirts and comfy pants over trendy clothing. Her shoulder-length wash-and-wear brown hair is cut straight across the bottom, softened by fringy bangs, and her only nod to style is a pair of gold wireframe glasses. But once you have the chance to see Jennifer in action, you realize that, despite any physical difficulties, with her quick wit, even temper, and her uncanny ability to be in the right place at the right time, there are no limits to what this Girl Scout leader and her troop can accomplish.

At the law firm and literary agency where Jennifer works as the office manager, her coworkers tease her by saying that she has 20 daughters—all the girls in her troop. And although she really only gave birth to two of them, her Scouts are truly like members of her family. Every weekend her black SUV is filled with girls going to badge workshops or working at community service projects like the annual cleanup of the antique carousel at Glen Echo Park, a local arts space. Zipping around town with a car full of girls is how Jennifer likes to spend her time because she always wanted to have children. But she knew she wanted a different life for herself and her family than she had as a small town girl growing up in Belleville, Illinois.

"Just turn back the clock 50 years and you're in my hometown," Jennifer says as muffled sounds of chatting and laughter from her daughters and their friends drift upstairs from their basement home in a large two-story house. "It's being pulled dragging and screaming into modern times. Buddy Epson is the most famous person to come out of Belleville. And he never moved back once he left. Neither have I. I'm from one of the few counties where the AFL-CIO had to build an office because it was suing it so much."

Jennifer came to the DC area in 1990 to work at an un-paid internship for her congressman. After trying to sur-vive for a few months on an allowance from her folks, she realized that she needed to find a job that paid enough to live comfortably in DC. She found a full-time job that fit her needs at the Capital Children's Museum, just a few blocks from her congressman's office on Capitol Hill.

"I liked my job at the Capital Children's Museum, so I stayed there for 10 years—until it closed" Jennifer says. During her early days working for the museum, Jennifer shared an apartment, and one of her roommates was from

Somalia. On weekends, the house would smell of cinnamon, sage, and clove as they cooked exotic dishes for a wide circle of her roommate's friends and family who conversed in Somali into the night. Sitting in her living room taking in the incense and good company, Jennifer fell in love with the Somali traditions and people. When she confided this to her roommate, "She tried to set me up with every single Somali guy she knew." After a series of single dates, Jennifer met Abdul. She found him charming and handsome, and he admired and enjoyed the company of the young woman from Illinois. They courted for just a few months, and then the Catholic girl and the Muslim man married in a civil ceremony and celebrated with Jennifer's new Somali family.

International customs and travel have always held an appeal for Jennifer because her mother, father, and three sisters all appreciated seeing new places. Her mother, a former high school French and Spanish teacher, traveled abroad with high school groups at least once a year. They even came up with a spreadsheet to keep track of how many states and countries everyone had visited.

"It became a big fight as to whether you could count the District of Columbia as a separate item. Miss America gives them a separate contestant, so we should put DC on the spreadsheet." Jennifer's point was taken so a trip to DC now earns family members a credit. Her sister was keeping the spreadsheet for a while; now Jennifer's taken over the official record keeper duties.

"The rules are that you can't count being in an airport as a visit, but you can count passing through on a train 'because you've seen the land.' This rule was decided upon one Thanksgiving twenty-something years ago." Her father, an attorney, made sure the rules were clear. Jennifer has gotten credit for visiting all but six states—Alaska, Hawaii, North Dakota, Oregon, Arkansas, and Nevada.

For family trips, taken when Jennifer and her sisters were young, her mom holds the institutional memory to get credit for each state. To receive credit for later trips, family members have to either send a postcard or take a photo in the state.

To get international credits, the rules for the family game are more complex. When they were in high school, Jennifer and her twin sister took a school trip to Germany where they flew into Berlin and then went to Munich by train. So, by the rules of their family competition, they can count East and West Germany. Their youngest sister went to Germany as an exchange student after it was unified so she can only count the unified country. "But," Jennifer says, "We told her if we go back we get to count unified Germany but you'll never get East and West Germany."

The game extended to new members once the girls started their own families. When Jennifer's Pakistani brother-in-law took her sister back to his country to visit, Jennifer's parents went, too. "Everyone joked that my parents went just to get the country on their spreadsheets, Jennifer says. "All of the grandkids also have their own lists, but there are specific rules there, too. My sister wanted to claim states they had visited when she was pregnant for her baby, and my mother ruled against it."

The first year of Jennifer and Abdul's marriage brought the birth of their first daughter, Amina, and the arrival of Abdul's father to live with the young couple. By the time she was one-year-old, little Amina had learned the basic posture and manner for worship, and she joined her grandfather in his daily prayers.

With the next year came the birth of a second daughter, Halima, known as Hallie. Abdul's father had returned to Somalia, but discord was the newest visitor to their household. By the time Hallie was a year old, Jennifer and Abdul had separated. Once she got divorced, Jennifer moved near the museum so that she could be close to work and the girls' babysitter. She found an apartment at Sixth and H Street NE, in a neighborhood that had seen its share of urban crime.

"I was close to everything I needed to be near. It was cheap and my next-door neighbor was a lady whose daughter also worked for the museum. So my neighbor tells me, 'If anybody gives you trouble, just tell them that you're a friend of my son's.' He was well-known in the neighborhood…a big guy who was the quarterback at Spingarn High School. I asked her what his real name was and she told me that nobody knew him by that name. I said 'If I'm scared, I not going to say I'm a friend of Boo's. I'm not going to do that.' So she explained, 'Everyone knows him by Boo.' Luckily I never had to pull that one out."

The top floor of the Capital Children's Museum was the site of the first DC charter school. The director of the museum, Jennifer remembers, told the DC Public Schools, "'Give us your worst… the kids that are at-risk of dropping out'…and they *really* did. We had 16-year-olds that were in the seventh grade. We had kids that had already had two kids themselves. I was relatively new to the area—the naïve country girl—and we all had to help out with something, so I helped with the TV production class, one of the classes that brought the kids to school every day. One day, when I was taking roll, I asked the kids in the class where their classmate Michael was. This was back when Reebok Pumps were popular and the kids said, 'Someone jumped him for his pumps…they stabbed him in the knee.' When I asked why they had attacked his knee—and this was the part that scared me—they said, 'There're no major arteries in the knee, so you can only be charged with assault, not attempted murder.'"

Jennifer's parents came up to visit her one summer during her time at the museum, and they drove over to Annapolis to see the sights. They were on their way back into DC when her mother decided it was absolutely necessary to stop for gas at that very moment. "It was eleven o'clock at night, and we were coming down New York Avenue in Northeast DC. So my father pulls over at the gas station. This was long before cell phones. My mother decides she also needs call my sister to let her know they were on their way. So I walk over to the payphone with my mother, which was right next to some bushes. My mother picks up the phone, and six guys come out of the bushes. My mother hangs up the phone and whispers: 'Go back to the car. Go back to the car.' I happened to turn around and one of the guys says, 'Hi, Miss Jennifer.' 'Hey Pedro,' I said. It was Pedro from one of my classes at the museum. We got back in the car, and my mother says, 'I'm not going to worry about you...you know all of the hoodlums in town.'

The charter school kids also figured out they could get out of school if they called in bomb threats because everyone had to evacuate the building. Jennifer was sitting in her office making arrangements for a teacher to visit the museum when she looked out of the window, and she saw that everyone else had evacuated the building and thought to herself, "Thanks guys, I'll just sit here and die at my desk." But the evacuations started happening so often that eventually, none of the staff bothered leaving the building during the threats.

Working in the museum gave Jennifer a solid foundation of knowledge that has been invaluable to her as a Girl Scout leader. In the museum was a child-sized chemistry lab, complete with lab coats and beakers with instructors that led children through simple experiments, an animation studio in which kids drew their own cartoon cells, a small replica of a Japanese subway car, and other hands-on exhibits.

"But the bus was my favorite... did I tell you about the bus? I was riding on the Sixteenth Street bus, and we passed another bus that had been hit in the back by a construction truck. The empty bus was just sitting there, and I wondered all day, 'What will they do with that bus?' We had a little lemonade stand bus at the museum that was made of wood. It looked like the Lucy Advice Stand from Peanuts with 'Bus' painted on it. So I started calling the transit company asking them what they would do with the part of the bus that hadn't been hit. It took a couple of months, but they finally said, 'We'd love to bring that bus to the Capital Children's Museum.' So they came and installed it. We had the real driver's seat and the fare box and every day you could find big and little kids at the steering wheel. They asked if we wanted them to hook up the horn, and we said "NO." After the museum closed, our bus went to the junkyard, but it was great while it lasted."

When the time came for Amina to begin Head Start, Jennifer decided to move to Silver Spring, Maryland, in Montgomery County. Montgomery County public schools are highly regarded nationally, and Jennifer wanted her girls to be enrolled in that school system. "When I was at the Children's Museum, I saw all of the schools, and I knew which ones I liked and which ones were 'no way.' And I liked the Silver Spring area." As the mother of biracial girls, she felt it was also important that they settle in a place with cultural diversity. Later, as a Girl Scout activity, Jennifer took the kids to see *The Great Debaters*, Hallie asked if people really treated black people the way it was portrayed in the movie. In second grade Amina did a report on Martin Luther King for King Day, and she said she was thankful to MLK because he made it possible for her mom and dad to get married.

Although she's been a Girl Scout leader for almost 10 years, and she is the only leader that Hallie has ever known, Jennifer only became a leader when the first troop she put Amina in turned out to be a bad fit. At that time Jennifer was spending her time and energy working with the PTA at her girls' school, where she got to know many of the families that are now part of her troop. When she realized that she had a different philosophy than Amina's troop leader about how a troop should be run—Jennifer thought the girls should have more input—she decided to give her time and energy to running a troop of her own.

After living in a few different places near the girls' elementary school, Jennifer and her girls found the perfect living situation sharing a house with another single mom and her daughter. "My roommate, Carlota, was going through a breakup and, without someone to help with the mortgage, she couldn't afford to keep the house. So we live downstairs in the basement, we share the first floor, and she and her daughter Pilar, who is in Jennifer's troop, live upstairs. We're still close to everything, and the girls were able to stay in the same schools."

Carlota, a college psychology professor, is also happy to share her space and her pets with Jennifer and the girls; the main floor that separates the two families allows everyone the space that they need. Wandering between Jennifer's family in the basement and Carlota and Pilar on the second floor are Bebe, a black cat who darts out of the door to escape whenever possible, and Rosie, a laid-back black dog, who is content hanging out under the feet of kids doing homework at the dining room table.

A striking woman of South American heritage, Carlota has long dark hair that cascades like a waterfall down her back. Her college teaching schedule is hectic during the school year but her summers are spent traveling with Pilar to Buddhist temples around the world. Carlota makes up part of what Jennifer calls the single moms' network, which provides support and respite for the busy working mothers.

Jennifer always has at least two kids besides hers in tow. "Even though I don't have family here, I can call one of the other moms and say I have something to do next Friday night. And vice versa." The girls' best friends go back and forth between houses. Hallie's best friend, Chanell, is also a member of the Girl Scout troop and her mother, Kim, is the troop's money manager.

Speaking with just a hint of a Jamaica Queens, New York, accent, Kim, a petite nutmeg brown woman with a head full of short springy curls, gives off a vibe that alternates between intimidating and sociable. Kim uses the same skills as the troop manager as she does in her work as an accountant for a group based in Florida that runs oil changing businesses in the South. She came to DC in her early twenties to find work where she met her husband. They divorced when Chanell was young.

Two deep dimples adorn Chanell's cheeks, and her braces flash as she giggles. When her daughter was in the third grade, Kim moved Chanell from public school, where she'd already started attracting attention from the little boys in her class, to a girl's Catholic school with uniforms. Now, with no boys to distract her, Kim has faith that the nuns will give Chanell the best education possible and that her daughter can keep her mind on her studies. For Kim, keeping Chanell on task means keeping close track of what her daughter does on the computer. Although the girl was forbidden to use Facebook, one of the other Scouts set Chanell up with a secret account. That secret came to light when the Chanell left a page open and her mother saw an instant message on the family computer.

"She was talking to some boy she met on vacation," Kim says." When I confronted her about it, she cried and told me that she'll never do that again," Kim says. "I talked to her about talking to strangers on the Internet, but I don't know how to keep her safe. She's on lock down now, but I don't know how long I can keep this up." Part of Kim's strategy is to keep Chanell busy, and Girl Scouts are part of that plan.

At the end of seventh grade, Chanell was given a full scholarship by the school. Kim felt it was a blessing from God and pledged to give as much time helping out at the school as her job would allow. She hopes that Chanell will get a scholarship to Spelman College, a historically black women's college in Atlanta. When Chanell goes, Kim plans to go there at the same time to finish her college education, like the mother-daughter duo in Mo'nique's television show, "The Parkers." Meanwhile, they come to Scouts as much as possible.

"We call them Ham and Cheese," Jennifer says playfully about Hallie and Chanell. "When the troop went to see the Harlem Globetrotters, it was no surprise that those two were chosen to come down on the floor." The girls met in Kindergarten where they bonded over trying to get out of having to read during reading time.

"Kim and I asked the teachers to please not put them in the same class again because they were feeding off of each other." Hallie, Jennifer explains, has an unidentified learning disorder that affects how much she can retain of what she reads. When she was being diagnosed for her learning disorder, which took over a year, the school brought in a psychologist who, although he had yet to meet Hallie, told Jennifer that she might need to prepare herself to accept that she had a low-functioning child. Jennifer told him, "If my child has been able to convince teachers for two years to not make her read, I'm going to say not 'low functioning.' Con artist, yes. The 'I'm hungry,' 'I'm tired,' 'I had a bad dream I can't get my mind off of it' excuses that teachers fall for… I'm thinking she's not at all low functioning."

Hallie's memorization was so good, it was hard for Jennifer to tell when Hallie actually learned to read. When she was little she loved hearing her mom read the book *Brown Bear, Brown Bear* over and over again. Jennifer grew so tired of reading it to Hallie that she hid it behind the book case. Hallie got construction paper—brown, yellow, and red—and made her own *Brown Bear, Brown Bear* book and "read" it because she had completely memorized the book.

When the psychologist told Hallie in second grade that they were going to do some reading, Hallie told him, "I only read pages with pictures." "People couldn't tell if she was reading or not because she was memorizing what went on page six," Jennifer says. "If a card had the tear, she knew what was on that card, but she couldn't recognize the same word in another deck."

Hallie's reading continues to be a challenge, but she's found more success as a math and science student. She also loves arts and crafts and helped design the troop's bright felt banner that they carry in parades and use to decorate the table during booth sales.

While Hallie is comfortable being creative, Amina is what her mother calls a natural safety patrol. "You tell her the rules," Jennifer says, "and she'll enforce them." In keeping with that, one of Amina's favorite parts of being a Scout is representing the troop in flag ceremonies. Jennifer put the troop on the list of Sudden Service volunteers. When there's a chance to do something out of the ordinary, like being part of a sporting event or representing the Girl Scouts somewhere interesting, she and the troop are ready to go. "They like to use diverse sets of girls that look like the Scooby Doo gang," Jennifer says.

"We've done flag ceremonies at the crack of dawn, it feels like, because they're starting at 8:00 a.m. on a Saturday morning, and I'll say we'll do it. Because if we do those events, they'll call us for the really cool things, too, because they know we'll show up."

One summer at the National Mall in Washington, DC, the girls passed out water at the rehearsal of the Annual Fourth of July Concert at the Capitol. "The girls wanted to know, 'What are we doing this for?' Then we got front row seats under the teleprompter, and we could even see Vanessa Williams sweat because it was so hot out there. To top it off, we got a picture with Gloria Estefan."

The troop families pitched in to buy Jennifer a new digital camera because she takes pride in documenting all of the girls' scouting adventures. "The girls know the routine now. At the end of every trip, I always get a photo to put into our troop scrapbook." She makes a big book to keep and gives each Scout a small one before they recess for summer so that they can remember all of the year's activities. "My old camera was slow, the flash took forever to recharge, and my batteries kept dying at the worst times. Now I can take twice the pictures in half the time," Jennifer says.

"I was in a commercial for Channel Nine news for a school supply drive," Amina says. "We had eight people talking saying donate supplies at Sun Trust Bank. It took about an hour to make the commercial. The commercial was only about thirty seconds, but it took so long to make because people kept laughing or missing words. My sister kept looking down at the paper when she was saying her lines, and you can't do that. I like being in commercials but I don't like talking in them. When I went back to school people kept saying, 'I saw you on TV.' I think it's kind of weird seeing yourself on TV."

Some of the girls in Jennifer's troop were in another commercial to promote buying Girl Scout cookies on Channel Four when they were younger. Decked out in their official uniforms, they sat in the hallways of the television station for a couple of hours until it was finally their turn to go into the studio. It was worth the wait though because they, along with another Brownie troop from Bethesda, did a short interview with Channel Four Meteorologist Veronica Johnson, and they got to be on set while she did the weather report. Then, as they were leaving, Little JJ from on a Nickelodeon television show, and Brandon, a young actor from the teen movie "Roll Bounce" came to talk with Arch Campbell, the movie critic at the station. "Miss Jennifer," the girls called out to her, "Where's your camera?" And they each got a souvenir photo with those celebrities.

Amina, who is usually dressed in clothes that will allow her to join a pickup game of basketball at any time, plays center for her middle school team and hopes to become a sports marketer so she can promote her favorite team, the Mystics. Her favorite memory of scouting so far was during Girl Scout Day at Six Flags when she first met her favorite basketball star, WMBA Mystics player Alana Beard. "I took a picture with her and I sent her a copy of the photo, and she sent it back autographed," Amina says proudly. "It's one of my favorite pictures because I was with my sister and my best friend. When I do flag ceremonies, at the Verizon Center, I see her there."

Amina also donned a large Thin Mint full body costume at one of the basketball games to get people's attention so that they would buy cookies at the troop's booth sales. She remembers how people stopped, waved, and took photos of her dancing around. "The Girl Scout Council has the uniforms that any troop can borrow," Jennifer explains. "It's worth the trip to get them because they bring people over to the cookies…and that's the whole point of a booth sale, right?"

And although Amina doesn't mind covering herself in heavy felt to sell cookies, her least favorite part of Girl Scouting is wearing the official uniforms. "I don't like the stiff khaki. You always have to wear khaki pants. I said the Pledge of Allegiance at the Capitol in front of Nancy Pelosi, and it was uncomfortable. You have to wear black shoes with the uniform, so I couldn't wear my basketball shoes. You have to walk around in those black shoes all day, you can't take them off. We were at the Capitol for a bill signing when that they increased the minimum wage twenty-five cents. I got to meet Nancy Pelosi and take a picture with her. To go to those kinds of things, you also have to wear the vest, and it's all heavy with all of the badges and the pins you have to put on it."

While meeting Congresswoman Pelosi was just one of many exciting scouting opportunities for Amina, Jennifer recalls that getting the photo was harder than her daughter remembered. "I ran after her saying, 'Ms. Pelosi, photo with the Girl Scouts?' I kept yelling through her security people and finally she looked around and came back to get her picture taken with the girls. She was really sweet and told them all that they'd done a great job." Some of the others well-known officials in attendance also took pictures with the girls. "While we were taking a photo, Ted Kennedy put his arm on Amina's shoulder, so she was really impressed with him," Jennifer remembers."

In between the flurry of activities that come with Sudden Service and the planned Scout outings, the troop meets twice a month on Wednesday evenings. "The meetings are not the best part of Girl Scouts because some people are tired and in a bad mood. Sometimes there's too much girl drama," Hallie says. The best part of the meetings for her is being with her friends. "A lot of my friends are Girl Scouts. My favorite memory about being a Scout is meeting all of my friends there and going camping with them." On a camp-out a couple of years ago, the girls were taking a night hike. All of the girls with flashlights moved toward the front of the line. "So my mom says, 'Give me some light back here' and suddenly a flash of lightning came out of nowhere. That really scared us. We all ran to the back to be closer to my mom."

Hallie also goes camping with some of her Girl Scout friends in the summer at residence camp. "I like going to camp in the summer at Camp May Flather," she says. "The first week at camp I did arts and crafts, the second week I did decorating clothes up in the lodge. The last week I got to ride horses. The first week at camp was my favorite because in the morning people were quiet, and in the afternoon they were hyper. That's how I am—quiet in the morning and hyper in the afternoon. Amina doesn't go to camp…she doesn't like any sleepovers. I don't like going to camp by myself, so I go with a friend." Last year Chanell went to camp with Hallie where they told all of the campers they were sisters and that their camp names (nicknames Girl Scout campers give themselves) were Mo and Coco. Chanell wasn't happy about the lack of flush toilets, and she got homesick after a week, so she's decided to skip camp for a few years.

"This year I'm going to camp with a younger girl—Kristine—and we're going to Camp Fabulous at Camp May Flather. I've heard it's like a spa and we're going to learn about nails and skin. That's what my mom says. My favorite camp song is "Tarzan." I'm like my mom…I like to sing loud," Hallie says and starts to sing:

Tarzan, was swinging on a rubber band,
Tarzan, smacked into a frying pan,
Ouch that huyts,
Now Tarzan has a tan,
And he hope it don't peel, Like a ba-nana."

Kristine, Hallie's new campmate, fit in immediately when she joined Jennifer's troop. The multicultural makeup of the troop was perfect for a little girl whose family is equally as diverse. Her mom, Shalen, grew up in Oregon and was a Girl Scout herself through high school. She had wanted to go to college on the East Coast, but Shalen's parents didn't want her to be that far from home. After graduation, however, Shalen finally had the chance to see what life was like on the other side of the country when she came to Washington, DC, to do an internship. While working for a nonprofit, her father passed away unexpectedly. Feeling that she needed a permanent change, Shalen decided to make the DC area her new home.

Her husband, Pat, came into Shalen's life when she was part of the DC singles' scene. Pat, an athletic guy who still rides his bike as often as possible, comes from a family that immigrated to the United States from Nicaragua before he was born. While they were dating, he took Shalen to meet his family in Brooklyn. It was there that she met his three-year-old niece Kristine, whose bubbly personality and big brown eyes drew Shalen to her.

With each trip to New York, Shalen grew more and more attached to the little girl, who was being raised by a number of relatives because her mother was seldom home. After Pat and Shalen married, Kristine asked if she could come live with them and their family was born. Now their family is complete with the addition of a baby brother.

In second grade, Kristine introduced one of her classmates to the troop when she invited Natasha to a Brownie meeting. At first the others didn't pay much attention to the younger girl but after seeing Natasha's beautiful artwork during a badge activity, she was enthusiastically welcomed into the group.

While the troop has its share of single moms, there are also a few single dads who dutifully bring their daughters to Scout meetings. "Three girls in the troop came to me and said 'Donnita needs Girl Scouts.' They told me that she needed the Girl Power." So Jennifer invited Donnita to join, and her dad signed the necessary papers. Now that they've moved to another county, Donnita's dad drives almost an hour each way, bringing Donnita and picking her up from meetings.

Samantha, better known as Sam to the Scouts, is also in the care of her dad, David, and he waits quietly every week at the side of the meeting hall for the girls to be dismissed. At first glance, it looks as though this big scruffy guy with the baritone voice has gotten lost amidst the soprano chorus of moms and girls. "I saw Sam at the bus stop the other day," one of the moms says about his tall blonde daughter, "and I couldn't help but notice how beautiful and grown up she looked. I'm sure she must have a lot of admirers."

"I just show the boys my collection of medieval weapons and they keep their distance," he says with a smile. He isn't joking about the weaponry. As a collector of authentic looking daggers and spears, he is a regular performer at the Renaissance Festivals. He's also demonstrated their uses to Sam's class and to the Scout troop, though most of the girls in the troop were more interested in his costume than his arsenal of knives.

Twelve-year-old Molly, the smallest member of the troop, has yet to break the five-foot mark and still weighs less than seventy pounds. Molly's mom, Amy, wasn't a Scout growing up, but she believes in girl empowerment and attended Mt. Holyoke College, a women's school, in the 70s. After law school, when Amy married, she and her husband struck a bargain that all of their sons would take his last name and all of the daughters would take hers. All three daughters proudly carry their mother's name. As the youngest of three girls, Molly followed her sister Rory into Jennifer's troop. When Rory began getting roles at their community theater, Amy told Jennifer that Rory would have to miss Scouts because play rehearsals were also on Wednesday nights. "Girl Scouts is never supposed to add stress to your year," Jennifer replied. "That," Amy says, "was exactly what I needed to hear." Now she chauffeurs Molly to as many Scout outings as possible. And although Molly is the smallest of the group, she is often the first one to put up her hand to vote for rough and tumble Girl Scouting activities like dog sledding.

Emily, who goes to the same school as Sam, is known as the sensitive Scout. At one troop camping trip, a daddy long-legs wandered into the tent, and one of the girls killed it. "That put her into tears, Jennifer says. "She told the other girls, 'It's their home, not ours.' And that really stuck with the girls, so now when we're camping someone will inevitably come up to me and say, 'Miss Jennifer, get rid of Emily, there's a bug in the cabin, and we've got to kill it!'"

Emily and Rory were in a play at a local theater that was a retelling of Shakespeare's "Love's Labor Lost," set in a 1930s traveling circus. Rory was a strong man with big muscles, and Emily was a mermaid. More than half of the Scout troop came to the play and waited out front after the show with an armful of colorful carnations to congratulate the thespians. "All of our neighbors who had kids in the show were really impressed that the Girl Scout troop came out to support Emily and Rory. And anyone who tells us that they're in something, we try to support them too. Not everybody goes, but it's enough to make the point."

Several members of the troop have been part of the group since Brownies. Jailand joined in third grade after hearing about the great activities the troop was involved in. Not one to sit around bored, Jailand is ready for any kind of activity—from spa weekends to creek cleanups. Her high energy level was a major factor in becoming one of the troop's top cookie sellers. Jailand sold hundreds of boxes of cookies after knocking on almost every one of her neighbors' door in her large apartment complex.

Naimani is Amina's basketball friend who came to check out the Girl Scouts and became a faithful troop member. Ife, who joined the troop in sixth grade, also heard about the troop from school friends. After learning about the troop's activities, Ife was hooked on Girl Scouting. Being a member of the group checked all of the boxes on her list: community service opportunities, being part of a supportive network of friends, and the chance to have fun.

The troop's diversity also includes members from other countries. Sabareeshini, whose family is from India, went to her homeland for a summer wedding and tried to convince her family to go to the Girl Scout center during her visit. "I don't think they made it," Jennifer says. "I don't know if she realized how far away it was and how big India is. Sabareeshini is one of our most serious and devoted Scouts. One winter when the ground was frozen with snow and ice, I had to cancel the meeting because the recreation department told me that the building was closed. Sabareeshini seemed crushed, and she wanted to know if we were going to reschedule."

Honey, another troop member with international roots, came to the United States from Eritrea when she was six. The oldest of three children, her days are spent in Catholic school and she splits her free time between studying and Girl Scouts. Whenever Jennifer has a Sudden Service opportunity—no matter how early they have to arrive—she can count on Honey to be ready to go with a smile on her face.

The troop has participated in all types of activities—fashion shows, service projects, bike rallies, learning to change a tire—but Jennifer's favorite was an overnight workshop held at the Annapolis Chesapeake Children's museum where students learn about the Underground Railroad. An actress who made the history real for the kids took on the Harriet Tubman role.

"She led the group outside and we took on the identity of runaway slaves who had to hide in the shadows," Jennifer says. "The museum must have asked their neighbors to walk their dogs because there was sniffing and barking all over the place. We were sneaking around quietly so that we wouldn't get caught making our way to safety at the Quaker House. Everyone was really into it. Then one of the girls who used to be in our troop stopped and said, 'Wait a minute, I'm white.' And I told her, 'Not tonight. Tonight you're a black slave. Now get down!' But the cool thing was that she had forgotten who she was and that we live in a different time. The director of that museum was great.

And, of course, she was a Girl Scout." ⚘

"Recently during a walk around my neighborhood, an older woman I'd never met before engaged me in conversation. As we were talking, another woman and a young girl holding a shopping bag of Girl Scout cookies came up to us.

'I need to speak with you,' the approaching woman said, getting uncomfortably close to my neighbor. 'My daughter says that when she tried to sell you cookies, you slammed the door in her face.' I stood by awkwardly, not sure if things might come to blows. The older woman assured the mother that she'd told the girl, from behind a closed door, that she didn't talk to strangers.

'I guess this is a teachable moment,' the mother said to her daughter, as they walked off, 'that not everyone wants to buy cookies.'

A few minutes later, the mother came back holding a box of Thin Mints. 'As a peace offering, my daughter would like to give you these cookies.'

'I don't eat cookies,' my neighbor said curtly and turned away.

Moments later, I left the scene wondering if the older woman—who initially had seemed so pleasant to me—had indeed slammed the door in the Girl Scout's face. After all, what kind of person could say no to a free box of Thin Mints?"

Monica Snipes

"Growing up in Brooklyn, New York, I was a Brownie Scout for one year. When Girl Scout cookie time came around, my troop decided we would use our money for a trip to Great Adventure Amusement Park in New Jersey. We were really excited about it and everyone sold as many cookies as possible. After the cookie sale ended, our leaders took off *with* the cookie proceeds. I was pretty young, but I remember there were a lot of whispers about what had become of them. And, of course, there were no more Brownie meetings after they left, so we never got to go to Great Adventure. I guess the leaders went off on a great adventure of their own."

Emily Epstein Landau

Cookies and Dough

Clap, clap, clap-clap-clap!

After giving the Girl Scout signal for "quiet down and listen up," Jennifer stands in the middle of the large room and waits for the girls in her combination Junior-Cadette troop to echo her clapped message. Instead of the expected response, however, she hears nothing but continued conversations and giggling. On this February 2008 evening where the outside temperature is still 65°, a touch of spring has brought a sense of restlessness to Troop 2288 that not even the Girl Scout call for order can subdue.

The girls moving around the room reflect the diversity of the Silver Spring area. This city, located just a few miles from the Nation's Capital, is home to black, white, and Hispanic residents who live side by side with those who've come to Maryland from around the world. The Scouts in Troop 2288, whose families speak English, Spanish, Amharic, Somalian, and Tamil, could easily be the girls shown on Girl Scout cookies boxes.

Even Jennifer's daughters, who usually see themselves as her helpers, are distracted today. In one corner, Amina dribbles and shoots her imaginary basketball. Her red, white, and blue Nikes squeal as she touches down from her throw onto the center's white linoleum floor. With her navy sweatshirt hoodie tied around her neck like a superhero cape, she cheers as she scores a point for her invisible team. Still wearing her satin jersey emblazoned with a navy blue number14, she re-enacts her middle school team's earlier victory on the court.

At the other side of the room, Hallie perches on one of the tables that line the walls of the recreation center and engages in a lively exchange with another troop member about school. Beneath her partially unzipped silver and white hoodie is a matching shirt, both of which complement her crystal-embellished jeans. Hallie's dozens of long braids, drawn into a thick ponytail by an elastic band, flip from side to side as she laughs with her friend.

"Quiet down, girls. Quiet down." Jennifer lets her gaze fall on the Scouts as she sends out a gentle reprimand. The room becomes silent and she repeats her call to order.

Clap, clap, clap-clap-clap!

This time the 11 girls in attendance for tonight's meeting answer her clapping with their own, some more enthusiastically than others. They settle into folding metal chairs, scoot up to a long oblong table, and await the night's agenda.

"Before you leave tonight, I need everyone to sign up to sell at our cookie booth sales," Jennifer says, pointing to papers taped to the table off to the side. "For those of you who haven't done this before, booth sales are fun—we set up a little store where we sell cookies. We have one sale later this month at Trinity College and the other one will be on Palm Sunday in front of the Blair Giant supermarket. If you can come, we really need your help."

The girls decided at the beginning of the school year to spend their cookie proceeds on a trip to the Treehouse Camp. Camping at this unusual site, located near Harpers Ferry, is an experience that most kids long for—sleeping seven feet off of the ground in large wooden tree houses. The cost for lodging, transportation, and food will be $50 per girl. With a current enrollment of twenty registered

Scouts, the girls must raise at least $1000. Since they will receive 60 cents for each box of cookie that they sell, every box counts.

Natasha raises her hand. Her serious expression sets the tone for her question. "Miss Jennifer, when do we get the cookies to give to the people who already ordered them?"

"I'm picking up all of our cookies on February 21, remember? That's a Thursday. You and your mom or dad should come get your cookies from my house Thursday night or Friday so that you can deliver them as soon as possible." Natasha scribbles down this information, so she can share it with her mother at the end of the meeting.

"Any more questions about the booth sales or the cookie pick-up?" Jennifer looks around and then proceeds. "Okay, tonight we'll be working on badges. We're going to do some forensic science to earn a badge called *Uncovering the Evidence*. The other badge is called *Cookies and Dough*. We've completed most of the requirements for the cookie badge, so that one should be easy. Especially since we know how much you all love cookies."

"First, let's do some fingerprinting." Jennifer holds up an official police department fingerprint card and an inkpad. "Over on that table are a bunch of these cards, some ink pads, and a container of baby wipes. Be sure to wipe your fingers off good or we'll get ink everywhere."

Without further prompting, the Scouts get up and start fingerprinting themselves. At the same time, Jennifer has each girl make a single print from her right index finger on a blank index card. She puts those cards aside to dry.

"Miss Jennifer, I messed up." Ife, whose pink sparkly T-shirt says *Head in the Clouds*, runs over to the leader and displays her set of defective prints. They are smudged and the ink on the paper is too thick to distinguish the arches loops and swirls found on her fingers. "Can I do another one?"

"Sure," Jennifer says, "Just slow down this time." Ife bounds back over to the table to try again as the other girls finish. She successfully captures her prints and settles back at the meeting table in time for the next task.

"Pass your set of prints to the left until I stop singing." She starts singing the Beyonce Knowles song "To the Left" and a few girls start to moan their displeasure.

"We can use my cell phone for music," Donnita suggests. She grabs her phone from her jacket, presses a button, and the phone starts to play a song.

"That's okay, Donnita." Jennifer gives a bemused smile to her critic. "I'm finished now so you can put your phone away. Girls, look carefully at the fingerprint card that you're holding."

Donnita reluctantly returns her phone to her pocket and, along with her troop mates, inspects the set of fingerprints that she is holding. Jennifer sets down the stack of small white cards with the Scouts' index prints on them.

"Now I want you to find the index card with the fingerprint that matches your big card." The girls dive toward the pile to grab an index card.

"This is hard," Chanell says. She stares intently at the index card she holds and seeing that it doesn't match, she passes it to Honey, who is sitting to her left. "Somebody, give me another card," Chanell says. After rejecting five or six cards, she finds the match and holds it up for everyone to see.

"That's great, Chanell." Jennifer looks around the table. "How about the rest of you?" One by one, the girls all find their matches and Jennifer nods approvingly.

"Okay, let's put away the fingerprints and move on to the cookie badge. It says in the badge requirements that we should think of new ways to market cookies. Does anyone have any ideas?"

Samantha raises her hand. "I read that the colors red and yellow make people hungry," she says. "Those are the colors that McDonald's uses. Maybe we should make our signs red and yellow for the booth sales."

"I don't like McDonald's," Pilar states flatly. Pilar is fondly thought of by the troop as their walking encyclopedia. She knows a lot about many things and has strong opinions on most subjects—this being no exception. Hallie laughs and agrees with Pilar. A flurry of cross conversation begins as the girls start to talk about their own opinions on McDonalds and other fast food restaurants.

"Are there any more marketing ideas?" Jennifer asks. "Sometimes good smells make people want to buy more food. I read that at the circus, they boil onions to make people hungry so that they'll buy more hotdogs."

"Miss Jennifer, how about if we give away some homemade cookies? They smell *really* good," Ife offers.

"I'm not sure that would help," Jennifer responds gently. "We're trying to sell Girl Scout cookies, so that would make us our own competition."

As the girls start to offer their own opinions on homemade cookies, Jennifer turns to a different cookie badge requirement.

"It says here that we have to poll at least 10 people about their favorite Girl Scout cookie. There are 11 of you here, so we're going go around the table and say what your favorite cookie is and why. Then I want each of you to make a chart so that we can see which is the most popular for our troop. Who wants to write down everyone's choices?" Honey and Pilar both volunteer for the job, and they each get a piece of scratch paper and a pencil.

"That's fine. You can both be the note takers. Let's start with Amina."

"I like Thin Mints 'cause they're chocolaty and they're minty," Amina offers.

Molly, the youngest of the Scouts, follows suit. "Me, too!"

"I like Thin Mints the best, too," Donnita says.

"Alright," says Jennifer, "how many of you like Thin Mints the best because they taste like chocolate and mint?"

Honey, Natasha, and Samantha raise their hands. Pilar and Honey note the popular vote for Thin Mints.

"How about you, Hallie? What's your favorite flavor?"

"I like Tagalongs. They remind me of Reese's Cups."

"Good. How about you, Pilar?"

Pilar carefully spells out her choice in American Sign Language. The whole troop learned basic sign language from their recent badge work, so they easily decode her choice as she fingerspells.

"A–l–l A–b–o–u–t–s. All Abouts," the girls say in unison.

"Why are All Abouts your favorite cookie?" Jennifer asks.

N–o–t t–o–o m–u–c–h c–h–o–c–o–l–a–t–e, she signs.

"I like All Abouts, too," says Ife. "*I like them because they are good*," she sings to the troop. The girls laugh appreciatively at her impromptu serenade.

"Ife, you're crazy," Chanell says. "I like Tagalongs. I like chocolate *and* peanut butter."

"That gives you the last word, Sabareeshini. What's your favorite?" All heads turn to the quiet girl as she makes her selection.

"My favorite," she says decisively "are the Do-Si-Dos. I like peanut butter, but I really don't like chocolate. So the best one for me are the peanut butter sandwich cookies."

"Good. So, Honey and Pilar, what's the final count?

"That's six Thin Mints, two Tagalongs, two All Abouts, and one Do-Si-Do," Honey reads off her paper as Pilar nods in agreement.

"Now, everyone take a piece of paper and a color pencil from the box on the table and make a chart that shows our favorite cookies. You can do any kind of chart. A bar chart, a pie chart, or any other kind of chart that you can think of. If you want, you can make it really colorful by using a different color for each kind of cookie. That'll make it easier to read. Once we're done, we'll compare them."

Each girl puts her own spin on her chart and after comparing them, it's clear that Thin Mints are Troop 2288's favorite cookie.

Kim, Chanell's mom and the troop's money manager, comes in to join the meeting. "So, what's the most popular cookie?" she asks.

"Thin Mints."

She shrugs her shoulders at the group's response. "What happened to Samoas? That's my favorite." She goes over to one of the side tables and leans against it.

"This year we've sold a lot of all the cookies," Kim reports. "Does anybody have a guess as to how many boxes of cookies we've sold so far?"

"One hundred boxes," is the first guess.

"Two hundred."

"Me and Hallie sold two hundred and sixteen boxes by ourselves," Amina says. "It has to be a lot more than that." Jennifer's daughters have decided to team up in their cookie sales this year so that they can win more incentives.

The theme for the current cookie sale is "Make it a Hit," so most of the prizes have something to do with music or being a star. By selling at least 12 boxes of cookies, most of the girls in the troop have earned the Make it a Hit patch for their uniforms. All those with sales of 36 boxes will add a light-up compact mirror decorated with pink and red stars to their bounty, while72 boxes sold will yield them all of the lower prizes plus a pink and silver star-studded black backpack. A black and white dog radio with a curlicue tail antenna is the additional prize for those who sell 110 boxes. For those who reach the 150 box sales level, a stuffed white Maltese-type dog that spends its time on a red velvet pillow will join their prize package.

Amina and Hallie have yet to hit the 225 box sales level, but for those who do, they will receive a baby-doll T-shirt that continues the star theme. The top prizes, the pink and white shower radio and the star radio pillow, will be added to the booty of those who sell 350 boxes and 500 boxes of cookies.

Hallie immediately fell in love with the dog on the pillow—that's the prize she's looking forward to getting. Amina still has hopes to earn the shower radio. That means that they will have to sell a lot more cookies at the troop's booth sales.

"Any more guesses about how many boxes of cookies we've sold?" Kim asks the group. "Well, here's the good news. Even before we start the booth sales, we've sold 988 boxes. At 60 cents a box, we've earned almost $600."

"Now you girls can see that we need to sell as much as possible at our booth sales," Jennifer adds. "Who wants to sign up now?"

With that good news, the Scouts run up to the sign-up sheet and write their names. Miss Kim's news of how well the sales are going energizes the group, and the noise becomes almost deafening. Jennifer decides that they've done enough cookies talk and badge work for the evening.

"Snack time," she says and calls for Natasha and Donnita to pass out the treats.

Within minutes, all that remains of the graham crackers are crumbs left on the table, and the juice pouches are completely flat and empty. Going to the trashcan to throw away their empty pouches has given most of the girls' excuses to start running around again. Molly whizzes around on her Wheelie shoes, and Sam follows in pursuit to pick up the smaller girl. Donnita, Ife, and Chanell start singing like *American Idol* contestants and Pilar puts her hands over her ears to block the noise. In the midst of the chaos, Natasha and Sabareeshini gather up stray color pencils and put them in the Scout supply box, while Honey gathers up loose papers and sweeps the floor.

"Mom, is it time to go yet?" Hallie asks. Amina stands by her side looking hopeful. Jennifer checks her watch—it is exactly eight o'clock. Some parents have come to pick up their daughters, and they're collecting flyers and permission slips for the next activity and waiting patiently toward the door.

"Girls," she says, gathering them back together. "Let's form a friendship circle. The girls make a tight circle, holding hands with their arms crossed right over left.

"Can I start the friendship squeeze?" Ife asks. This old Girl Scout tradition brings the meeting to a close. Everyone is silent as the friendship squeeze is passed around the circle. The squeeze stands for friendship among the Scouts.

"Sure." Ife squeezes the hand to her left and the pulse goes around until everyone has had a chance to pass on the good wishes. When Jennifer gives the signal, everyone lifts their arms and twists to the right until they're facing the outside and drops hands.

As parents retrieve their daughters, Jennifer reminds them about the cookie pickup on February 21. She gathers the troop supplies and has Hallie and Amina take them out to her car, where they will stay until the next meeting. It's been a busy night.

"Let's go, Mom." They are tired and ready to go because *America's Next Top Model*, one of their favorite television shows, has already started. Jennifer sets the alarm at the front door, turns off the overhead lights, and together they walk out into the warm February night. ❧

"I trace my love of ice skating directly back to a long ago Girl Scout cookie sales season. When I was in sixth grade, my Junior Girl Scout troop decided that we would use our cookie proceeds to pay for ice skating lessons. We knew that the more cookies we sold, the more lessons we could afford so we sold to everyone we knew. As I recall, we sold enough cookies to get instruction and practice time on the ice every weekend for at least a month. Those lessons at the U-Line Arena in DC were great, and I got good enough to make my way around the ice.

While I was never Olympics bound, every four years I'm glued in front of the television watching the American figure skating team compete. I also love watching all levels of ice hockey, both in person and remotely. Although it's been years since I felt the ice beneath my feet, I appreciate the technique and skill of competing skaters because of what I learned during those lessons funded by my troop's cookie sales."

Pamela Myrick

Cooking With Cookies

"**E**veryone, look at the meeting table and tell me what you think we're going to do today," Jennifer says to her troop.

With that, the girls begin an impromptu march around the table to examine the items before them—three bunches of slightly green bananas, two quarts of large strawberries, a carton of fresh blueberries, a gallon of whole milk, a block of cream cheese, a large can of whipped cream, two bags of mini-marshmallows, a stick of margarine, two quarts of vanilla ice cream, a can of evaporated milk, one large bag of milk chocolate chips, and a container of Cool Whip. Stacked at each end of the pile of food that runs the length of the table are boxes of Thin Mints, Tagalongs, All Abouts, Do-Si-Dos, Samoas, and Trefoils.

"Are we having some kind of party?" Kristine asks as she cuddles a bag of mini-marshmallows that she's claimed from the mound of food. Another troop member grabs the bag from the younger girl and puts it back on the table.

"I guess you could call it a party," Jennifer says. "One thing's for sure, we'll have lots of good things to eat when we're done. Today we're going to use Girl Scout cookies to make different recipes. Kind of like the Iron Chef TV show. Has anybody watched Iron Chef?"

"It's a show on cable where two chefs compete to see who's the better cook," Pilar answers.

"We're not going to have a contest today," Jennifer says, "but we are going to do something else that they do on that show. We're going to use the ingredients on the table to make a lot of different things...and all of the recipes must include at least one kind of Girl Scout cookie."

"Why are we going to do that?" Natasha asks.

"Well, when we sell the cookies at the booth sale, you can tell your customers other ways that they can use the cookies besides just eating them right out of the box."

"That's the best way to eat them, though," Sabareeshini says.

"True," Jennifer agrees, "but just in case anyone asks, you'll have some good suggestions about what to do with leftover cookies." She picks up several sheets of paper and shows them to the girls. "These are recipes that I got off of the Internet, but you can use your creativity to improve on them or even make something totally different. Here's an interesting one," she stops for a moment and then looks up at the girls. "Who wants to make Samoa Chicken?"

The Scouts' faces contort with horror as they think about the combination. "Ewwwwwwww. Gross," they say.

"That sounds disgusting," says Emily. The eight-grader, who led the troop in yoga exercises at an earlier meeting, has been a semi-confirmed vegetarian since grade school. Jennifer smiles at the troop's strong reaction.

"It's a good thing you don't want to make that one, because I didn't bring any chicken. How about Thin Mint Milkshakes? Does anyone want to make those?" The girls brighten at this idea and almost all of them put up their hands to volunteer.

"Okay, Honey, Naimani, and Molly. You go over to that table," Jennifer points to a table by the door, "where the blender is."

Honey picks up a carton of ice cream, the milk, and the recipe. Naimani and Molly each take a box of Thin Mints, and the girls walk over to their workspace.

"Oh, and don't forget to put a tablecloth down before you start, Jennifer instructs. "Otherwise, we're going to be here all night cleaning up." Molly gets a red plastic tablecloth from the supply table and the milkshake chefs get to work.

"The next recipe is," Jennifer reads off of the next piece of paper, "S'mores made with All Abouts. Who wants to make those?"

The girls jump up and down and wave their hands in the air to be chosen.

"Sabareeshini and Hallie," Jennifer says handing them the recipe. "You go into the little room over there with the microwave." Without having to consult the paper, the two girls scoop up the mini-marshmallows and the All About cookies and skip over to the room to begin cooking.

"Next we have Cheesecake with a Trefoil cookie crust. Who wants to make that?" The girls silently look around at each other. "I guess we won't be making that recipe," Jennifer says as she puts the sheet of paper back on the table. "Too bad, I like cheesecake. I guess I'm the only one. How about Tagalong Balls? Does that one sound good to anybody?"

"What are they?" Emily asks.

"They're candy made from ground-up Tagalongs. Kind of like Reese's Cups, except softer and round. It's all explained in the recipe."

Kristine and Natasha, two of the younger Scouts, raise their hands for the chance to make this treat. "You two, take your ingredients and go over to the table with the food processor, right next to the Thin Mint Milkshake group." Jennifer hands them the recipe.

"It says here that we need peanuts," Natasha says, reading the paper, "and I don't see any peanuts on the table."

"I think they'll still be good without peanuts," Jennifer says. "You can choose something else from the table to add to the recipe if you want to."

Kristine and Natasha pick up a box of Tagalongs and the bag of chocolate chips and go back to their station.

Pilar, Donnita, Ife, Amina, and Emily wait patiently for their assignment. Jennifer picks up another recipe. "Is anyone interested in making All About Trifle?"

"What's that?" Donnita asks.

"Here's the recipe," Jennifer says, handing it to her. "First you make vanilla pudding and cut up fruit like those strawberries and bananas. Then you put several layers of pudding, fruit, and All About cookie crumbs in a cup and top the whole thing with whipped cream." Donnita holds onto the recipe and starts picking up the boxes of pudding.

Pilar volunteers for trifle duty. Jennifer points her toward the small kitchen area to begin making the recipe. Pilar takes the whole milk, a box of All Abouts, and the fruit to their area.

"That leaves you, Emily and Amina. I have some more recipes here if you don't want to join any of the other groups."

Amina closes her eyes and says that she's too tired to cook today. Then she puts her head down on the table.

"How about you, Emily?"

"I'm going to make up my own recipe from Tagalongs and marshmallows."

'That sounds good," Jennifer says. "Let me know if you want me to help you with anything." Emily takes a box of cookies and the marshmallows to another table and begins working on her cookie creation.

As the girls at each station work, Jennifer talks in hushed tones with Amina. Once she is satisfied that the best thing to do for Amina is to give her some space, the leader begins visiting the various workstations to see how the troop is faring with their culinary challenges.

At her first stop, the milkshake table, Honey has just blended the first batch of ice cream, milk, and Thin Mints. The first-year high school student has taken the lead in this group. She pours the light brown concoction, dotted with dark specks of chocolate cookie, into a plastic cup. Then she takes a sip and passes the cup on to Molly and Naimani for them to taste and offer their opinions.

"It needs more ice cream. I *told* you it needed more ice cream," Naimani says as she digs a large spoon into the carton and scoops more ice cream into the blender. Honey and Molly agree that the shake is indeed too thin and Honey pushes the button on the blender again. It whirs for about fifteen seconds and then she pours a good-sized sample of the modified recipe. All three girls agree that more ice cream has made the milkshake thicker and better. Jennifer leaves the group as they pour the remainder of the mixture into two cups and start making the next batch of shakes.

As she approaches their table, Jennifer sees that Kristine and Natasha have already put an entire box of Tagalongs into the food processor. She is just in time to help the girls twist and push the machine's lid down until it locks into place.

"The food processor won't work unless the top is on just right," Jennifer explains.

The girls take turns pushing the buttons, as the cookies are transformed from round discs to a fine paste that looks like cookie dough. The ground-up Tagalongs stick to the sides of the processor and to the blade at the bottom of the machine.

"This is so much fun," Natasha shouts above the machine's loud hum. "I love cooking."

"Let's put in the chocolate chips now," Kristine says as she rips open the bag. She pours in half of the chips and the two girls get the processor lid to fit this time. Again they take turns pushing the buttons and the chocolate chips disappear into the Tagalong dough.

"Can we taste it?" they ask Jennifer when they're done.

"Sure."

They twist the lid off of the processor bowl and each girl digs a plastic spoon into their creation.

"Delicious," Natasha declares and Kristine nods in agreement.

"Now to make the Tagalong Balls," Jennifer says, looking at the recipe, "Spoon balls of the mix onto a sheet of wax paper and then put them into the refrigerator for a while to harden."

Kristine gets the box of wax paper from the supply table while Natasha picks up several clean plastic spoons. After laying out the paper, they each get a heaping spoon of Tagalong-chocolate chip mix on their spoons and try to transfer it to the wax paper. The Tagalong dough clings to the spoons.

"I can't get it off," an exasperated Natasha says. "What should I do?"

"Take another spoon and scrape it off."

The girls take the leader's suggestion and this time they get the mixture off their spoons and onto the wax paper. However, they are not pleased with the way their recipe is turning out.

"Miss Jennifer, I think we still need the peanuts to cover the balls like they have in the picture that goes with the recipe," Natasha says, pointing to the paper. "Our Tagalong balls don't look right."

"Since we don't have any peanuts, can you think of anything else that you can roll the balls in?"

Natasha and Kristine go over to the table to see what's left, but nothing strikes the girls as the right ingredient to use to coat the Tagalong Balls.

Jennifer offers them a suggestion. "How about if you crush up another kind of cookie and roll the balls in cookie crumbs?"

They dash back over to the meeting table and decide to add Trefoils to their recipe. Natasha brings the cookies back to their station, while Kristine gets a couple of zipper-lock sandwich bags from the supply table, brings them back, and hands one to Natasha. They put Trefoil cookies into the bags and smash them against the table over and over again until the butter cookies are pulverized into fine golden crumbs. Natasha pours her crumbs onto a paper plate, then Kristine plops a Tagalong Ball into the pile of crumbs. After rolling it around until it is fully covered and placing it on the wax paper, both girls declare their first Tagalong Ball to be acceptable. Jennifer agrees and leaves them as they start the process again.

Emily has several of her cookie creations lined up on a wax paper sheet when Jennifer walks over to check in with her. She has broken Tagalong cookies into halves and placed each half onto a bed of mini-marshmallows. Then she microwaved them just long enough for the marshmallows to soften, expand, and cling to the cookies. The resulting product is a confection that looks like half-moons sitting on clouds of mini-marshmallows. Seeing this resemblance, Jennifer suggests the name Tagalong Clouds, but Emily had already christened her recipe Marshmallow Wafers. Emily carefully moves a sheet of her creations to the freezer and then begins work on the next set.

After checking in with Amina, who's beginning to show some interest in participating in the night's activity, Jennifer goes into the room where Sabareeshini and Hallie are making S'mores. Unlike the traditional S'mores, which are composed of graham crackers, Hershey Bar squares, and marshmallows, tonight's recipe calls for the Scouts to substitute All Abouts Girl Scout cookies, a round vanilla cookie that's coated with chocolate on one side, for the crackers and chocolate bars. The recipe calls for the cooks to sandwich four or five mini-marshmallows between two All Abouts, chocolate side in.

"Mom," Hallie says, "We've made more than a dozen S'mores, but certain individuals keep coming in to try our recipe."

Sabareeshini adds, "They're so good right out of the microwave."

Jennifer assures them that since the cookie treats are so popular, the cooks must be doing something right. She lets them know that there are plenty of cookies and marshmallows so there will be S'mores for everyone who wants them, now or later.

"Keep up the good work, she says as she moves on to see how the Trefoil Trifle group is doing.

Pilar and Donnita have put the finishing touches on their first parfait as Jennifer peers into the rec center's small galley kitchen. She picks up the clear plastic cup to admire the alternating layers of pudding, whipped cream, and a mixture of strawberries, bananas, and blueberries.

"Where are the All Abouts," Jennifer asks.

"We decided not to put them in," Donnita says.

"I guess that's alright, but I thought we were thinking of ways to serve the Girl Scout cookies tonight."

"We thought it would taste better without them," says Pilar.

"Well, your trifle looks good, with or without cookies. Why don't you girls let me take a picture for our scrapbook of you and your creation?" The troop leader gets her camera and Pilar and Ife, an unofficial taste tester, pose for a shoot with the finished dessert.

"Miss Jennifer," Donnita says, "what should we do with the rest of this stuff. We still have a lot of fruit and pudding."

"Make some more trifle. We need enough for everyone to get a good taste of your recipe."

The girls open up the second box of pudding, dump the powder in a bowl, and add a cup of milk. Donnita stirs the yellow goop to make it thicken. As Pilar comes back into the kitchen, Donnita complains that she didn't have the chance to do enough with the first batch of trifle.

"You cut up the fruit, made the pudding, and put the whole thing together. It's my turn to make the trifle now," Donnita says.

Pilar pushes her black wire frame glasses up on her nose, looks hurt for a moment, and then shrugs her shoulders. Without a word, she puts on her coat and walks out of the center's front door to go home. Jennifer, making the rounds taking photos of the girls with their cookie creations, notices that Pilar is gone.

"What happened to Pilar?" she asks Donnita.

"She got mad and went home," the girl responds matter-of-factly. Jennifer picks up her cell phone and calls Pilar's mom to tell her that her daughter is on her way.

"It's fine," she says to the girls. "Pilar's mom will make sure that she's home safely." Jennifer finishes taking photos of all of the groups for the troop archives and then she calls for the Scouts to bring all of their creations to the meeting table. Natasha and Kristine get their Tagalong Balls from the refrigerator, and Emily retrieves her Marshmallow Wafers from the freezer. Molly, Honey, and Naimani transport several cups of Thin Mint shakes to the table as Hallie and Sabareeshini bring out plates of the All

About S'mores. The girls sit down at the table and admire all of the sweets that they've made with Girl Scout cookies.

"Donnita, come join us," Jennifer says.

"I'm still stirring the pudding," she calls out from the kitchen.

The girls pass around plates and everyone samples the goodies. Even Amina has livened up after eating a plate full of sweets.

"These are good," Natasha says as she eats a S'more.

Jennifer gets a plate and compliments the girls on their efforts. "I really like Emily's Marshmallow Wafers," she says. "And these Tagalong Balls look kind of interesting," she says, "but they taste amazing. Everything is really tasty." Jennifer takes another sip of milkshake.

"Miss Jennifer, what are we going to do with the leftovers?" Naimani asks.

"I guess you can take them home." Naimani rushes over to the S'mores and puts a few more on her plate to save for a later snack.

"Ife, which of these treats did you help to make?" Jennifer asks.

Ife grins as she eats a spoonful of trifle. "I helped with all of them. I was the taster."

"That's true," Honey says. "Ife helped us taste the milkshakes."

"And the S'mores," Hallie adds.

"And the Marshmallow Wafers," Emily offers.

"And I think she even tasted the Tagalong Balls," says Kristine.

"I tasted everything," Ife says, "and I can say that everything is delicious."

Donnita comes out of the kitchen and asks Jennifer if she can make a special cup of trifle for her father. Seeing that everyone has filled up on the rest of the treats, Jennifer says yes. With this news, the girl goes back into the kitchen, and brings out a parfait cup of trifle, swirled high with whipped cream and dotted with blueberries.

"Mmmmmmmmm. That looks good," Naimani says, eyeing the dessert cup.

"And it's for my dad," Donnita informs her.

"Let's clean up," Jennifer says and the girls go to their respective stations to start wiping up crumbs and spills.

"Do we have to wash the dishes?" Honey asks, looking at the blender pitcher.

"Just put everything in that box on the supply table," Jennifer says, pointing to a large cardboard box, "and I'll take them home to wash." Molly puts the pitcher in the box, while Naimani and Honey throw away the tablecloth and wipe down their table.

Kristine's mother comes to take her home, and the girl proudly takes her over to see the leftover Tagalong Balls. As other parents arrive, the girls display their plates of cookie creations and offer samples of the goodies. Natasha walks around the room picking up copies of several recipes so that she can try making them at home.

Before locking up for the night, Jennifer makes her final inspection of the workspaces. In the room with the microwave, a few mini-marshmallows remain in one of the corners.

"Let's get those up," she says to Sabareeshini and Hallie and the girls grab the broom to sweep them up. "Remember," Jennifer says, "a Girl Scout always leaves places cleaner than she finds them." ❧

"My niece has learning disabilities and very little confidence. As we went door to door selling cookies with our Girl Scout troop, she wouldn't speak for the first twenty minutes due to her speech impediment. But thanks to our awesome leader's encouragement, my niece came out her shell and began talking to homeowners and selling like a champion. She went from zero confidence to being a great seller! Our leader brings out the best in all of her Scouts."

Beth Ramage

A Banner Day for Cookie Sales

"Girl Scout cookies! Get your Girl Scout cookies!"

With gray skies threatening rain on a chilly Palm Sunday afternoon in March, a steady stream of shoppers goes in and out of the Silver Spring Giant grocery store, some to do their weekly shopping and others just to pick up a few items. Even the busiest of them can't help but be drawn to the colorful display of Thin Mints, Samoas, Do-Si-Dos, Trefoils, Tagalongs, All Abouts, Lemon Chalet Cremes, and Sugar-free Chocolate Chips neatly arranged on a table under the supermarket awning in the Blair Apartment complex by Girl Scout Troop 2288. Once they catch potential buyers' eyes, troop members Natasha, Kristine, Jailand, Hallie, and Sabareeshini attract customers to their booth sale by calling out to them and holding up boxes of Girl Scout cookies.

Booth sales like this one are held throughout March during Girl Scout cookie season, wherever the council can get permission to hold them, which includes strip malls and upscale shopping complexes. Scouts are assigned to their sales locations through a lottery—the earlier the cookie manager registers for a booth sale, the better their territory and timeslot. These sales are an integral part of the cookie operation—60 percent of all cookies are sold through booth sales each year.

Jennifer has already loaded 25 cases of cookies into her Honda SUV and, with the girls' help, unloaded them at the curb to set up the cookie station in front of the store's exit doors. She rests against a stone pillar a few feet off to the side of the action and prompts the girls as needed.

"Girl Scout cookies! Get your Girl Scout cookies! Girl Scout cookies! Get your Girl Scout cookies!" Sabareeshini says over and over in a sing song to amuse herself and attract potential patrons. Her long dark braids move from side to side as she bounces around.

"Try counting to ten between the times you invite people over to buy cookies," Jennifer advises. "That way you won't annoy anyone."

The girl silently mouths "One-two-three-four-five-six-seven-eight-nine-ten," and then calls out again, in hopes of bringing more cookie buyers over to the table. A young woman in a denim miniskirt coming out of the store heeds the Scout's call.

"How much are they?"

"$3.50 a box."

"I'm trying to remember the kind I like," she says as she picks up boxes and examines them. "They have peanut butter and chocolate in them."

"That's the Tagalongs," Jailand says.

Jailand hands a red box of Tagalongs to the woman as she fishes a $5- bill from her purse and asks, "Do I have to pay tax?"

"No ma'am," Jailand says as she hands the woman her change—two quarters atop a limp dollar bill.

"Thank you,' the girls say in unison and several of them call out again to shoppers coming and going, "Girl Scout cookies!"

Those who come over to buy cookies can't help but take notice of the cheerful china blue felt banner that completely covers the cookie table. Multiple rows of cookies are stacked on the top half of the banner and the bottom, draped in front of the table and flowing to the ground, proclaims in large light blue handstitched letters: *Girl Scouts 4-Ever—Troop 2288*. Bordering the neat lettering are three rows of large felt girls holding hands like cutout paper dolls. This banner, created and painstakingly stitched by Jennifer a few years before when the troop marched in the Downtown Silver Spring Thanksgiving parade, is also decorated with a variety of patches that mark the troop's activities throughout the year, such as hostessing at the White House Easter Egg Roll and participating in the Girl Scout Sing-Along on the National Mall in DC.

Each felt girl on the banner represents a member of the troop. Using a spectrum of felt that ranges from light tan to dark brown to make the banner Scouts' faces and hands, each felt girl also sports a unique hair style and colors, including representatives with long black yarn braids, a brown pixie cut, yellow ponytails, and black corn rows. They have their own styles of clothing, too, but all of them are clad in felt versions of the standard Girl Scout vest, complete with badges. As folks hurry toward the entrance of the Giant, both the felt and real girls beckon to potential buyers to take advantage of the cookie sale.

An older gentleman walks slowly past the table while looking longingly at the cookies.

"Would you like to buy some cookies?" Hallie asks.

"Shoot!" he says, "I almost made it past y'all without buying any. They're not that good for me, but I just can't resist them." He picks up a green box of Thin Mints. "I'll take these," he says. "I'll have one after dinner every day 'til they're gone. I just can't resist these cookies," he says as he hands over his money.

"Thank you," the girls say as he walks away. They look around for their next buyer. Another customer makes her way up to the table and picks up a couple of boxes of cookies.

"What are you girls going to do with the money that you earn selling cookies?" the woman asks.

The girls' minds seem go blank, so they look over at Jennifer for the answer. "Remember the camping trip we're taking in May?" she reminds them.

"That's right, we're going on a camping trip in May," Kristine says.

"In tree houses," Natasha adds.

"And we're going white water rafting," Hallie offers.

"That sounds great," the woman says as she gets change from Sabareeshini. "Have fun."

"We will. Thank you." Suddenly, the table is crowded with buyers and each girl is helping a customer make their cookie choices.

"How are we doing for change?" Jennifer asks Jailand, who is keeping track of the bank.

"I think we're doing okay," she says. "We still have lots of ones."

"That's good," Jennifer says. "Sometimes we have problems when everyone gives us a twenty. That's what happens when people get their money from ATMs. They only have twenties."

"I'm cold," Hallie says after the cookie rush dies down.

"It is pretty cold out here," Jennifer says as a couple of the girls rub their arms to warm them. "I guess I'll go get some hot chocolate if Kristine's mom doesn't mind staying with you by herself."

Shalen, Kristine's mom, gives her a thumbs up and Jennifer walks around the corner to the Caribou coffee store to get the warm beverages. A man wearing a stylish dark suit with a dried palm cross sticking out of his breast pocket comes to the table to make a selection.

"Hello, little ladies," he says. "What kind of cookie do you have that doesn't have any chocolate in it?"

"The Trefoils don't have any chocolate in them," Natasha says.

"Okay, one box of Trefoils. How much are they?"

"$3.50 a box."

"Have mercy," he says with a shocked expression on his face. "When my daughter sold cookies, they were less than a dollar for each box. Times sure have changed."

"Do you still want them?"

"Of course. I've got to support the Girl Scouts." He looks at the box of cookies, shakes his head, and mutters under his breath, "$3.50 a box!"

"Is that a lot of money for cookies?" Natasha asks her mom, Rhianna, who has come to bring her a warmer jacket.

"I think it's about as much as any other cookie in the store," Rhianna replies. "Besides, our cookies are for a good cause, right?" Satisfied with this answer, Natasha goes back to straightening and arranging boxes of cookies on the table.

"We need more Thin Mints," she says and Kristine scoots under the table to pull cookies out of the cardboard cases stored below. Just her hand is visible as she puts five boxes of Thin Mints on the table.

"Do we need anything else while I'm under here?"

"We could use some more Do-Si-Dos," Jailand says glancing at the table, "and a few more Samoas."

Kristine hands the cookies to the girls and stays under the table. "It's warm under here," A couple of the girls begin to make their way under the table as Shalen stops them.

"Kristine, come out from under that table before you get hurt," she says. "The rest of you girls, make sure that the table still looks neat so that customers can see all of the types of cookies when they come up buy them."

"Hi. We'll take two boxes of cookies," a middle-aged couple says as they select a box of Samoas and Tagalongs."

"That'll be $7," Sabareeshini says. The woman looks into her wallet and, seeing that she has no cash, asks her husband for the money. He reaches into his pants pocket, pulls out his wallet and finds that he, too, has no money.

"Oh well, sorry," he says. "Maybe next time."

"They could have gone to the bank machine for money," Jailand says once they're out of earshot. At that moment, Jennifer arrives with steaming paper cups of hot chocolate and the lost sale is forgotten. She hands each girl a cup, and they all sip and slurp it eagerly.

"This says Oreo hot chocolate," Natasha says reading the black marker writing on her cup. "I don't taste any Oreos." Rhianna squints her eyes and gives her daughter a look that stops her complaints.

"Eww. This tastes like coffee," Hallie says. "Mom," she says to Jennifer, "you know I don't like coffee!"

"If you don't like the way it tastes, then you don't have to drink it," Jennifer says. Hallie takes a few more sips and throws the cup in the trash. Shalen looks at her watch and reminds Jennifer of her tennis date this afternoon. "You've got everything under control?" she asks Jennifer as she heads toward her car.

"Sure, go ahead. I'll bring Kristine home when we're done."

A couple of college students, braving the cool weather in shorts, hoodies, and flip-flops come close to check out the cookies. "I want some Samoas," the guy says, as he balances a large bakery box on the table.

"It's not like we don't already have a whole cake to take to the party," his girlfriend says. On the cake, the message

Congratulations Hoyas is written in blue frosting beneath an illustration of a spirited bulldog dunking a basketball.

"I still want Samoas," he says, "And I'm not sharing with anyone."

"Fine," she says, as he pays for the cookies and they walk to their car with their sweets.

"Brrrrrr! I'm cold," Hallie says, rubbing her arms for emphasis. Her fleece jacket has proven no match for the gusts of March winds. Natasha's mom unzips her black leather jacket and hands it to the girl to put on.

"Thank you *so* much," Hallie says, snuggling into the jacket.

"Would you like to buy some cookies?" Jailand asks a woman walking behind the table pushing a double stroller holding a toddler and an infant.

"No thanks. I don't need them, and they're too young to eat them," she says, pointing to her children. "Good luck anyway, girls."

"Are any of these cookies sugar free?" a gray-haired lady asks as she looks over the stacks of cookies.

"The Sugar-free Chocolate Chips are what you want," Hallie says.

"Good. I'll take a box. I can eat those without putting my sugar out of whack." She pays for the cookies and continues to her car with her bag of groceries across her arm.

"What's does she mean when she talks about her sugar, Mom?" Natasha asks.

"You know, Sweetie, diabetes."

"Right." She turns and talks to Kristine "My aunt is a personal trainer, and she teaches us all about nutrition. Me and my mom always read the nutritional facts before we buy anything. We're into healthy eating." With that, Natasha picks up a box of Do-Si-Dos to read about its nutritional makeup. "This has a lot of sugar and fat in it," she says with a slight frown.

"That's because they're cookies," Rhianna reminds her. "Not too many cookies are good for you. That's why we don't eat them every day."

"Maybe that's why Girl Scout cookies aren't available all of the time," Natasha concludes. "Otherwise, everyone would eat them all of the time and get really fat."

"How much are the cookies?" a middle-aged man with a full dark mustache asks the girls.

"They're $3.50 a box. Would you like to buy some?" Sabareeshini asks.

"Not today," he says, "but I do want to give you some money so that you can give cookies to some people who can't afford to buy them." He reaches into his wallet, pulls out a $20 bill and gives it to the girl.

"Wow! Thanks," she says.

"We have a charity that we're giving cookies to," Jennifer explains. Looking at the girls, she asks, "Who can tell this gentleman what charity we are supporting this year?"

"The Rehab Hospital?" Sabareeshini and Jailand say in unison.

"That's right. The Girl Scouts have a program called the Gift of Caring," she says to the man. "Nice people like you give us the funding to donate cookies to a charity that the girls choose. In the past we've given cookies to the Ronald McDonald House, and this year we're giving cookies to the National Rehabilitation Hospital."

"Great," he says. "Good luck, girls, and thank you for doing nice things for others."

"Thank you," the group responds.

A young boy about six who's dressed in his church clothes—a gray pinstriped suit and a polka dot tie—runs up to the table waving a $5 bill.

"Hold on, Robert," his mother says over her shoulder as she pushes her cart in the other direction, beckoning the boy back to her side. "I told you that you could buy some cookies *after* we're done shopping." The boy's mouth takes a downward turn as he moves away from the table and slowly walks to his mother's side. They disappear around the bend as they go into the store.

"We need more Tagalongs and Lemon Chalets," Sabareeshini says as she surveys the table. Hallie checks the inventory below the table.

"That's the last box of Lemon Chalets," she says as she places a few more boxes of Tagalongs on the table. "We only have a couple more Tagalongs down there too."

"Good," says Jennifer, "The more we sell, the fewer we have to take home…and sell later."

"Girl Scout cookies! Get your Girl Scout cookies!" Sabareeshini says again.

"You're really into selling this year, Sabareeshini, aren't you? That's great. Last year, we could barely get you to talk to the customers."

Sabareeshini smiles shyly and calls out to customers again.

Grocery carts roll by, but none of the shoppers are interested in cookies. The girls sigh in boredom. Then a young woman walks up to the table with a clear mission in mind. She picks up one box of cookies and then another, reading the ingredients carefully. As she moves down the line of cookies, a lady with the grocery cart full of food moves in and grabs a box of Lemon Chalet cookies.

"Have you got any more of these?" she asks.

"No. I'm sorry, that's our last box." Kristine says.

"Darn, I wanted more Lemon cookies. Well, I guess I'll just take this one box then," she says.

"That'll be $3.50."

The woman hands Kristine her money and asks if there is any chance that more Lemon Chalets will be delivered.

"That's it, unfortunately," Jennifer says. "That's a new flavor this year. We're never sure how many to order of the new ones. I guess that the Lemon cookies are a hit."

"That's for sure," the woman says. "I would have taken five boxes if you had them." She put the cookie on her cart, and she and her husband roll it into the parking lot.

A black sedan pulls up and the driver calls out of the passenger window, "Do you have any Samoas?" The girls get him a box of cookies and take his money in payment.

"That's cool," Jailand says, "our first drive-through customer!"

"I'm proud of the way that you all have shared the banker responsibilities today," Jennifer notes. "Every time I look up, someone different is making change. I can see that all of you are working hard today. Now it's time to take the photos for this year's calendar," she says, getting her camera out of her bag. "Line up behind the table."

Sabereeshini gives the table a quick straightening and then joins the rest of the girls behind the table. Jennifer takes a photo.

"Smile, Natasha," she prompts and the girl breaks into a grin. "Perfect," the leader says as she shoots a few more for good measure.

"I can never walk by a group of beautiful Scouts." A tall African American woman in a dark blue suit and a shiny purple minister's collar looks admiringly at the girls and the cookies. "I can tell that you're all beautiful inside and out. Now, tell me what's the best kind of cookie?" The girls each gave her a suggestion as she gathers one box of each variety from the stacks in front of her. "That's seven boxes of cookies," she says." How much do I owe for all of these?"

"Seven times $3.50," Jailand says as the other girls silently go to work on this mental math problem. "You owe us...$24.50."

The lady hands her a $20 bill and a $5 bill. "Keep the change, "she says.

Her husband whispers to Jennifer what a big fan his wife is of scouting. "She can never walk by a Girl Scout cookie sale," he says as his wife hands him the stack of cookies to carry as they walk away.

"She bought seven boxes of cookies. That's our biggest sale today," Natasha says as she puts the money in the box.

"If you think that's something, you should have seen us when we had our sale at the subway station, right, Mom?" Hallie says.

"That's true. We sold a lot of cookies at the Silver Spring Metro station. Commuters love to buy cookies."

"How come we don't go back there?" Kristine asks

"Well, even though I got permission from the station master—I even have a photo of him buying a box of cookies, mind you—we found out later that it's against the rules to have a cookie sale outside of the subway station. And do you know what gave us away? This banner! If I hadn't had the banner on the table, they never would have known that it was our troop selling cookies that day. Then, I heard that a Baltimore troop came down to this area and sold cookies at the subway and they didn't get into trouble. Go figure."

"But we've sold a bunch of cookies today, though, so this is a good sale, too, right?" Hallie looks at her mom for confirmation.

"Definitely. How many cartons with cookies in them are under the table now?"

"We've got about 10 cartons left all together," Kristine says, after taking count. She pulls the empty cartons from under the table and puts them to the side.

"I'll take a box of those peanut butter cookies, please." The little boy in the gray suit is back, grinning as he waves his money in front of the Scouts. Jailand hands him a box of Do-Si-Dos while his mother stands with her groceries as he pays for the cookies. With his box of cookies in hand, he skips off contentedly with his mother to the parking lot.

"My feet are *so* tired," Jailand says, looking down at the concrete. "It feels like we've been here a long time."

Hallie agrees. "How much longer are we going to stay here, Mom?"

"We got here at one and it's about 2:30 now," Jennifer says. "We'll be leaving about 3:00."

"I've got an idea," Hallie says and she gets two empty cartons, turns one upside down, and fits one into the other. She sits down slowly on her new stool to test its strength. Satisfied that it won't collapse, she stretches out her feet. Kristine looks over at Hallie and gathers her own boxes to follow Hallie's lead. Soon all of the girls are relaxing on their makeshift chairs.

A lady in a long black wool coat rushes over to Jennifer's side and looks at her expectantly. "I'm here to get my cookies."

"Sure," Jennifer says. "We have plenty of cookies left. What kind can we get you?"

"I already ordered them," the lady informs her, "and paid for them. Eighty boxes. I was told that I could pick them up here. Today."

"I'm sorry, *who* told you that you could pick up eighty boxes?"

"The woman who sold them to me. She said that I could pick them up at the Silver Spring Giant this afternoon. So here I am."

"Maybe they meant a different Giant," Jennifer suggests. "There are a couple more stores in Silver Spring. We're the only ones here right now and, unfortunately, I don't know anything about your cookie order. Do you have the name of the person who sold you the cookies?"

The lady opens her purse and sifts through it to find her contact's name. "That's it," she says with a heavy sigh, closing the purse. "I'm never going to do anything like this again. I brought an order form to my office, collected the money, and sent it in. We were supposed to get the cookies delivered a couple of weeks ago. Everyone's been asking 'Where are my cookies?' So I called the lady who was supposed to bring the cookies—she's a former coworker's neighbor—and she said that I could pick them up today. Here."

"There was another Scout troop here this morning," Jennifer says. "Maybe they have your cookies. I will be happy to sell you more cookies, but I'm afraid that you'll have to take this up with the one who took your money." The lady shakes her head and picks up a box of Trefoils off of the table.

"I'll just take this box then. After all this time, I've been looking forward to having some of these cookies. Who would have thought it would be this complicated?"

Jennifer writes something on a piece of scrap paper and hands it to the woman. "Here's my number. If you can't find the person who sold you them to you, call me and we'll do some detective work. I'm sure we can track down your cookies."

The woman thanks Jennifer, puts the slip of paper in her purse, and walks to her car while dialing her cell phone.

"Goodness," Jennifer says to Natasha's mom, "Can you imagine how much of a hassle this is for her?"

"No kidding," Rhianna says. She looks around at the five Scouts perched on their cookie carton stools. "Do you think it's time to call it a day?" she asks Jennifer.

"I think so. We've done a great job selling, girls. Let's pull all of the cookies out from under the table and get things ready so we can load up the car." Rhianna stands with the group as they get up from their seats to pack up their cookies and supplies, and Jennifer goes to get her car. It takes some maneuvering but they get the utility table, banner, and most of the cookie cartons into the back of the car, with only a few cartons ending up on the backseat.

"Squeeze in, Jennifer says to Sabareeshini and Kristine, as Hallie climbs in the front seat."

"I've got to wait here for my mom to pick me up," Jailand says as Natasha and her mom go into the Giant to do some shopping of their own. "I called her and she'll be here in a few minutes."

"That's fine. We'll wait for her. In the meanwhile, hop in."

Jailand sits on a corner of the back seat as a woman rushes up to the car. "Am I too late?" she asks, looking at the cartons piled high. "Are there anymore cookies left? I saw that you were leaving, and I thought I'd blown my chance to get some cookies today."

"Not to worry," Jennifer says. "I can always make time for Girl Scout cookie lovers." ❧

Cookies and Camping

I t isn't supposed to rain in May. April Showers bring May flowers, Jennifer thinks as she searches the Internet to see what weather will be like the next weekend for the troop's mid-May camping trip. As she feared, the prospect for a wet weekend is undeniable: 80 percent chance of rain.

At about twilight on Friday evening, the four-car caravan of Scouts and their parents reach the Maple Tree Campground. As they traveled the hour-long drive from Silver Spring to Rohrersville, a rural Maryland town right on the West Virginia border, grey skies stretched out before them with only faint pink and orange streaks of fading sunlight sneaking through the clouds. The driver of the first car had almost missed the small wooden sign posted a little way back from the two-lane highway, obscured by overhanging lush green tree limbs. Just in time, Kristine's mom, Shalen, spots the sign and the entrance gate, and she signals the cars behind her. The cars turn right onto an uneven gravel road, stop to check in at the camp office, and carefully navigate the narrow twisting path up to the section of the park they'd reserved many months before.

Back in September when the girls planned the camping trip, the idea of sleeping under the stars in wooden cabins built around trees seemed like something out of a picture book that their parents might have read to them at bedtime when they were little. Most of the girls were convinced that this would be the ideal way to spend their cookie money. The year before, the troop had gone to Great Wolf Lodge, a comfy hotel attached to an indoor water park. That trip had been really fun, but this year the girls wanted to do something more "Girl Scout-like"—which meant roughing it in the woods. When Jennifer told the girls that this outing would include white water rafting, even troop members who had bad experiences with latrines and spiders from past camping trips were sold on the idea.

Now the cookie sales were done, the proceeds were accounted for and spent, and the troop had made it to the campsite. The cars pull into the parking area, and the drivers barely have the chance to shut off their engines before the girls jump out to stretch their legs and investigate their weekend home. They shine their flashlights into the campsite entrance where a cool fog, which seems to come from the trees, and a light rainfall form a misty veil in front of them. In the center of the camping area is a large fire circle where they will cook most of their meals. Picnic tables sit off to the side. Tonight they won't have to worry about preparing dinner. They'll eat whatever their parents packed for them—mostly sandwiches and chips—because Jennifer hadn't been sure how long it would take for the group to get to the campground. The girls set down their backpacks in the clearing, sit down at the tables, and quickly eat their brownbag suppers.

"Let's go figure out where we're going to sleep," one of the girls suggests when they're done, and they all race toward the cabins spread out on the property. The girls had already decided who they would be sharing a cabin with—that matter had been hashed out back at an earlier troop meeting. Now that they are actually on the camping site, each group needs to choose the cabin that will suit them best. As they move around and investigate the options, they can see that some cabins are larger than others. Inside of the cabins are between six and ten double-decker wooden sleeping shelves—that meant that the groups with the most members would get the largest structures. After sorting that out, the Scouts get their duffle bags and suitcases out of the cars. Once they make up their spots by carefully placing sleeping bags, blankets, and pillows on their chosen bunks, they set out stuffed animals and other touches from home.

Kristine looks around at her cabin mates who are lying on their bed, trying to get comfortable. "It's kind of spooky in here," she says. "Let's go see what everybody else is doing."

"Does anyone want to build a fire?" Jennifer asks the girls who've gathered out at the fire circle. Most of the wood in the main pile is damp, but she'd spotted a few dry logs under one of the cabins. It seems a shame, she thinks, not to have a campfire the first night of their outing. That is part of their tradition. The girls jump up and down at the mention of a fire, and a few start looking around for kindling.

"Can we make s'mores, Miss Jennifer?" Donnita asks, once the fire is going. The rest of the troop look at their leader expectantly.

"Of course!"

The Scouts scatter to find the perfect sticks to roast marshmallows on—long and a little green so that it will not catch fire as they attempt to toast marshmallows to a perfect golden brown. "Don't wander too far...and stay with a buddy!" Jennifer calls after them.

With their stomachs full of graham crackers, Hershey bars, and gooey marshmallows, the tired Scouts split up and go to their cabins to get ready for bed. They'd begun their mornings turning in homework and rushing from class to class and as soon school had let out, they'd traveled to this spot in the woods. The transition from city to country and from student to Girl Scout had left them in a state of exhaustion. After a few trips down the hill to the camp bathrooms (where most of the girls are relieved to find flush toilets), the Scouts get in their beds to sleep. Jennifer and the other parents check in to be sure that everyone is settled in, and then they go to their cabin to rest up for a busy weekend.

What had started out as delicate drizzle soon becomes driving rain that drums and thumps on the metal tree houses roofs while the girls try to sleep. Around 3:00 a.m., a crash of thunder joins the showery soundscape and jolts them awake.

"It's leaking in here!" Samantha cries out, shining her flashlight toward the center of the lodge. Their cabin is built around a maple tree and at the point where the tree and the roof meet, a small stream of water flows into the lodge and pools on the rough plank floor.

"Shhhhh," Emily whispers, pointing to their friend Molly who is sleeping soundly despite the thunderclap and Samantha's outburst. "Glad I didn't choose that bunk in the center."

"What are we going to do about it?" Samantha asks." I only brought one pair of hiking shoes."

"I guess it gets wet in here every time it rains. Just get your stuff up off the floor before it gets soaked."

Samantha puts her things on an empty bunk and hops back in the bed. "Great, she says, "It would have to rain while we're here. I told you we should have gone back to Great Wolf Lodge."

ᘒᕼ

"I'm cold," Chanell says from her bunk beneath Hallie. She chatters her teeth for effect. "It's too cold in here. I'm going to go sleep with my mother in the leaders' cabin."

"Don't do that...everyone will think you're a big baby," Hallie advises. "Here," she says, handing down an extra blanket to her friend, "You can use this. I don't need it."

"You know," Chanell says, "I heard that this is the same place where they filmed the Blair Witch Project. That was for real, you know. There really is a witch that snatches up kids in the woods."

"No, there isn't. And this isn't where that movie was either."

"Yes, it is. I heard Donnita and the rest of them talking about it. That witch is in Burkittsville, Maryland, and we're just a little bit down the road from there. I bet that witch can go wherever she wants."

"You're just trying to scare me." Hallie sweeps her flashlight around the cabin.

"No I'm not. I'm just glad there's a lock on the door."

"Me, too."

"I wonder what she does with them?"

"Who?"

"The witch. I wonder what she does with the kids when she catches them."

"Shut up and go to sleep," Hallie says as she turns off her flashlight.

The morning air holds a chill, and the rain comes down at a steady pace. About seven o'clock, girls begin to come out of the cabins dressed in warm clothes and covered in plastic ponchos. Some Scouts have come prepared with heavy gauge camping ponchos that could stand up to a storm, and others are covered in light see-through plastic ponchos like the ones tourists buy at Disney World during cloudbursts. All of them wear colorful kerchiefs or baseball caps to protect their heads from ticks.

"Who's hungry?" Jennifer asks with less enthusiasm than usual. She moves slowly toward the picnic tables. Her night's sleep had been interrupted when her daughter, Amina, knocked at the door around the time of the thunder clap. Amina's back started hurting from sleeping on the hard wooden bunk. To give her daughter some relief, Jennifer made herself into a human back rest by propping Amina up on her folded legs. Once she was comfortable, the girl had fallen back to sleep, but after hours of not being about to move around, Jennifer's legs are aching.

"We're having pancakes for breakfast with turkey bacon and scrambled eggs, right?"

"That's right. Luckily there's a charcoal grill here that we can cook on. It would take hours to start a fire this morning in the fire circle. And Miss Kim is going to do most of the cooking, since it's a little more dangerous. Who's setting up the table?" A few girls raised their hands. "Get the plates and forks ready and those of you who are cooking can mix up the Bisquick for the pancakes and hand Miss Kim the Eggbeaters and bacon."

"What should I do?" Ife asks. This was her first camping trip with the troop.

"You're on clean up, right?" The girl nods her head. "After we're finished eating, you and your group clean up and take the trash to the dumpster. That way animals won't get into it. We don't want any raccoons coming to visit, do we?"

Kim uses fire starter to get the charcoal burning, and she blows intermittently on the flames to keep them going. The orange flickering soon becomes a mass of red embers, and it is time to cook. With a careful choreography of pancake turning, egg stirring, and bacon flipping, breakfast is ready. The Scouts line up to fill their plates and then set them down on the yellow plastic tablecloth that covers the damp picnic table.

As the morning progresses, the rain becomes misty again. With ponchos still wrapped around them, the girls wander around the unit during their free time between breakfast and lunch. Most investigate what they hadn't been able to see in the dark the evening before. Lunch requires no cooking—the troop had chosen to make deli meat sandwiches. As they sit around the table, Jennifer talks to the girls about water safety rules, because it is almost time to go whitewater rafting.

"Can I wear my sweatpants on the raft?" Pilar asks. "I'm cold. It's too cold today to wear just my swimsuit."

"I guess you can," Molly's mother, Amy, tells her, "but they're going to get soaking wet. To be truthful, you'll be colder with the pants on because they'll get really heavy and uncomfortable." Amy and her family go rafting often, so she knows a lot about the sport. She's planning to rent wetsuits for Molly and herself, she tells the girls, because the river water is still very cold in the spring. "If you're too cold, maybe you should rent one, too." Pilar looks as though she might consider it.

"Who else besides Molly has been rafting?" Jennifer asks. A few hands go up. "Any more advice you can give to the girls who've never done this before?"

"Don't stand up," Kristine offers. The girls laugh and agree.

"Listen to the raft guide," Sabareeshini says.

"I didn't know you'd been rafting before," Jennifer says to the girl.

"I haven't. That's just common sense." Everyone laughs again. Sabareeshini is always the voice of reason.

"You'll get the full rundown from your guide, and I think you'll have to watch a movie about raft safety before you go. Any questions? Okay, then go change into your swimsuits—you can put clothes on top—Miss Kim and I will watch them while you're on the raft. Don't forget your towels!"

"How come you're not going with us?"

"I don't mind cooking and keeping track of cookie money," Kim says, "But I'm not much for water sports."

"I'd never be able to stand up when we were done," Jennifer answers. "It's just as well. Somebody has to watch your stuff."

The long white River Riders bus pulls onto the campground property at 1:00 p.m., and the girls and adults get on. The converted school bus could barely fit through the gate, but the camp manager directed it toward the opening where the Scouts were waiting. The sky is still overcast, but the rain had stopped. The bus bumps up and down the streets on the way to Harpers Ferry, where the rafts begin their journeys, crossing the state line from Maryland, to Virginia, and finally into West Virginia. As the time comes closer for the rafting trip to begin, some of the Scouts are feeling mixed emotions.

"What if I lose my glasses?" Amina asks her mother. "I can't see without them."

"I don't think they'll come off... that safety strap around your head that will hold them on."

"I don't know if I can do it," Natasha says. "Maybe I'm too little to go on the raft."

"I doubt it," Kristine says. "If Molly's not too little, then you'll be fine."

"I can't wait," Molly says. "Rafting is the best."

The bus pulls into a parking lot and the girls look around for the rafts. A guide explains that this wasn't the river—first the girls will get their flotation jackets and watch the training film. Then they will get back on the bus and go down to the river. The group steps off of the bus and almost on cue, bright sunlight breaks through the clouds.

"It's a miracle!" Kim says as she stretches out her arms and lifts her face toward the light. The girls laugh and some follow her example. Kim, Jennifer, and the other moms eye each other with relief about the weather's steady improvement, hoping that the sun might bring warmer temperatures for the girls' ride down the river. After such a dismal weather start to the camping trip, it looks as though things might be turning around.

Decked out in orange safety vests over their swimsuits and shiny navy blue helmets, the rafters are easy to spot. The bus lets the girls out at the top of a long flight of stairs that leads to the river. Once they make it to the bottom, the Scouts can see the final stretch of the Shenandoah River, which downstream joins with the Potomac River at Harpers Ferry. At this launching point, the wide expanse of river appears gentle, but it's understood that, further out, their two-hour adventure will become more challenging. The rapid currents are certain to toss the buoyant rafts around. As the girls head toward the river, an air of apprehension moves with them.

"Are you sure this is safe?" Jailand asks her group's guide as they take the rafts to the water's edge.

"I haven't lost anyone yet," the tan young woman in the River Riders jacket assures her.

Resolved to experience whatever comes next, the girls set their rafts into the water and get aboard. One after the next, the rafts leave the shore and glide to the center of the river while the girls paddle on command. Jennifer and Kim stand on the shore, waving and taking photos until the rafts were barely visible. Once they are out of sight, the women walk back up the steps and take the bus back to the River Riders offices to relax and wait for the Scouts to return.

About 4:00 p.m., the bus driver summons them to head back to the river. As they ride over, they wonder how the more timid Scouts have fared. There hadn't been any emergency calls that one of the girls has freaked out in the middle of the trip, so that was a good sign. And because there are Girl Scout moms on each raft, Jennifer and Kim are hopeful that all has gone well.

"Wait here," the bus driver tells them when they come to the same spot where he'd dropped off the girls. "They'll come up the stairs and meet us here. It shouldn't be more than a few minutes," he says as he walks toward a cluster of fellow drivers. The women wait for 15 minutes and start to get antsy. Where are the girls? Where is the driver? They find him in an animated conversation down the road. He assures the woman that it will be only a few more minutes. They hang over the rail to the stairs and wait. Finally, they spot a large group outfitted in orange flotation jackets coming up the steps.

"How was it?" Jennifer asks.

"It was fu-u-u-u-n!" Jailand says.

"It was really cool," Amina tells her mom. "I can't wait to do it again!" The girls around her nod their heads in agreement. Even the girls who are visibly cold—including Molly with her chattering teeth and her blue-tinged skin—have nothing but good things to say about the raft trip.

Sabareeshini beams with pride. "I was nervous, but I did it!"

Back at the campground, after the girls take showers and change into warmer clothes that will see them through the evening, there is a collective whine that everyone is *starving*. Jennifer opens the ice chest that holds dinner and the girls who signed up to cook take their places chopping carrots, broccoli, onions, peppers, and potatoes for packet cooking—roasting individual foil packets on the campfire. Chicken, tofu, and cheese are also on the menu. Everyone heaps what they like to eat into their packets, so no two meals are the same and no one is disappointed. Dessert follows with the choice of banana boats—bananas, chocolate chips, and marshmallows also cooked in foil packets—or more s'mores.

Darkness envelopes the Maple Tree Campground as the Scouts gather around a roaring fire. As is the troop's tradition, each girl writes a special wish on a paper strip, wraps it around a stick, and throws it into the fire. Jennifer writes a wish and throws her stick in last.

"Does anyone want to share their wish?" Jennifer asks.

"I wished that nobody had to go hungry," Emily volunteers.

"I wished for no more rain this weekend," Amina says.

"I wished for an Ipod," Ife says. "What did you wish for, Miss Jennifer?"

"I wished for health and wealth—and many more days camping under the stars with this troop." ❧

"Girl Scout cookies were a favorite among people sending care packages to soldiers in Iraq. But desert heat isn't kind. By the time the boxes reached us, the cookies with chocolate coverings had often melted into a giant single uber-cookie. But when they did arrive intact, the Thin Mints disappeared first. Loading our Humvees for patrol, we'd toss the unopened sleeves into the ice water in the coolers. And as we cruised through the Baghdad suburbs, the sunlight blinding white and the temperature well past 120 degrees, we'd munch on those crisp, icy reminders of childhood, a stack of Thin Mints swiped from the freezer door on lazy summer afternoons."

Brian Mockenhaupt

PART FOUR

National Perspective

Cookie Spin

FOR IMMEDIATE RELEASE – Lynchburg, Va. (January 13, 2009)

Peanut Corporation of America (PCA), a peanut processing company and maker of peanut butter for bulk distribution to institutions, food service industries, and private label food companies, today announced a voluntary recall of peanut butter produced in its Blakely, Georgia processing facility because it has the potential to be contaminated with Salmonella.

The timing couldn't have been worse. Only a few days before, Girl Scouts around the country had burst like horses from the starting gate, going to door to door with their order forms at the start of the 2009 winter cookie sale. Parents rushed to be the first to tack forms onto company bulletin boards from Washington state to Washington, DC. Enterprising Scouts sent out emails to grandmas and neighbors, describing the tastiness of the new cookie flavors and reminding their potential customers about old favorites like crisp, cool Thin Mints.

Now it seemed like news of the peanut butter recall was all that you heard about on the news. As jars of Jif and Peter Pan were being hurled into the trash, it was clear that two of the best-selling Girl Scout cookies—a peanut butter and chocolate patty on a cookie, and an oatmeal cookie sandwiched with thick sugary peanut butter—could see sales crumble. Michelle Tompkins, the Girl Scout national spokeswoman, had dealt with public relations nightmares before. But this was the first time that cookie spin was necessary at the beginning of the sale.

At the Girl Scout Headquarters, news of a possible peanut butter catastrophe began with whispers a few days before the story officially broke. As the whispers became louder, it was inevitable that the peanut butter crisis would begin to affect cookie sales. Pushing through the crowds and Fifth Avenue traffic, Michelle flashed her ID at the bank of security officers at the front desk and pushed the elevator button for the fifteenth floor. As she reached her office, she waved away her assistant Jeff and sat down at the computer to check her RSS feed. Were there any stories that linked the peanut butter recall and the cookie sale? Not yet. As she headed for the coffee station, Jeff told her about a strategy meeting to get a handle on the peanut butter crisis. The office pulsated with tension as Michelle quickly poured her coffee, went back into her office, and shut the door. Time to get to work and shut this one down. Was this what she thought she'd be dealing with when she came to work with the Girl Scouts? There had been a time, years ago, when she couldn't wait to begin her Girl Scouts adventures.

ঽ৶

"When I was a seven-year-old Catholic school girl, I joined the school's Brownie troop. We were allowed to wear our Brownie uniforms to school, so it was really special. On my first day as a Brownie, the troop meeting got canceled. My mom was a teacher at the school, so I ran out of my class, up to her seventh-grade classroom and into her arms. And I wailed 'There's no Brownies today!' The tears were horizontal."

During her own Girl Scouting days, Michelle was never a top cookie seller but she did her share of selling cookies to her family and neighbors. And her mom is still a loyal cookie customer. "My mom to this day still buys 12 boxes of shortbreads, freezes them, and takes two cookies out every day for dunking in milk and coffee. She makes them last the whole year unless someone goes and grabs them and eats them and then it's...kiss of death. You'd rather be dead first than eat her shortbreads. Well, we got a funny complaint letter from a guy a little while ago, asking us to get rid of the shortbread cookies because he believes that the parents who give their kids shortbread cookies don't really love their children." Michelle laughs. "Well, some people love shortbreads. My mom...she would take him down."

Originally from Sacramento, California, Michelle took a nontraditional route before she came to New York to attend Columbia University. After high school graduation, she was hired for an entry level job at a radio station. Her big break came when a deejay called in sick, and she got to go on air in his place. Although she decided that she didn't want to work behind a microphone, she liked the idea of finding employment for fledgling celebrities, so she found her next job at a local talent agency. "That prepared me to work with all kinds of difficult people," she recalls. "Then my parents bribed me to come back home and go to school. I enrolled at a community college when I was twenty-seven."

Although it had been a while since she'd been in a classroom, her real-world experience as a deejay and a talent agent gave her a strong foundation for her studies, so she excelled. Michelle had been on the dean's list every semester, and when she was about to finish, her academic and journalism advisers told her that she was shooting too low in the schools that she was applying to. She didn't want to go to any of the University of California campuses because her father taught business classes there, and those schools didn't seem like the right fit for her. She'd been in California all her life, so she decided to look at colleges on the East Coast. New York City had always seemed like a great place to live, so she sent in an application to Columbia.

"Three months later I got in. When the Columbia acceptance note came, my dad wrote a multi-colored note and posted it on the door."

Michelle came to Columbia in the fall of 2003, despite being told by all of her California friends that she was crazy to move to New York so soon after the September 11 attacks. But living in New York was just the kind of change that Michelle had wanted. Her film and anthropology classes were great, and hanging out in the city was a welcome change of pace from the Sacramento lifestyle that she was used to. The stately buildings of Columbia became her new home.

"After Columbia, I worked at a market research firm writing TV trivia questions and also freelancing. I got tired of tracking down money so I began to look for a full-time job. And then I started with the Girl Scouts as a temp, got hired three months later in the communications department, and then was promoted about a year later to the position that I have now."

Being a Californian transplanted in New York isn't easy for most, but Michelle seems to fit right in. With her shoulder-length dark hair and biting sense of humor, Michelle reminds you more of Brooklyn native Rosie O'Donnell than California girl Cheryl Crowe. And like many New York business women, she favors wearing black from head to toe, year round.

As the National Spokesperson for the Girl Scouts of the USA, anticipating what the public wants and needs is a key part of Michelle Tompkins's duties. And she's good at her job. As she sees situations develop, she has to be ready to respond to small issues like the temporary shortages of popular cookies and to potential sales disasters, such as the peanut butter crisis. During cookie season, there are more than 400 media calls each week, and about 300 of them are about cookies. Not that the Girl Scouts call it a cookie sale. They prefer to call it the "Girl Scout Cookie Program" and avoid referring to it as a sale at all because, Michelle explains, "It's really about what the girls are learning... it's about the goal setting, the skills, and they really get a lot out of it.

Although the National Office communications staff talks to the press about national trends in cookie sales while troops are busily selling in a fall or spring sale, there is less interest in constant tracking of what is selling and what isn't. Not surprisingly the largest councils, what Michelle calls the "big media markets," tend to have the biggest sales. The bottom line is that they expect that over 200 million boxes will be sold nationally each year, which will bring in more than $700 million dollars. The councils get a lot of their operating funds from the cookie program so for them it's crucial that it's a successful effort.

"People who know a lot about business say that at 60 cents a box, the return is fabulous. Look at Starbucks—they do not make that much per cup of coffee. That's one of the Girl Scout cookie myths, too; everyone thinks that all of the money from cookie sales stays with the National Office. Other than the licensing and fees, the money all goes to the local councils and the troops. The National Office is funded through Girl Scout dues. The licensing fees come from the bakers."

The communications department receives more than their share of letters every day—the mail cart delivers an average of 400 complaint letters from dissatisfied consumers each month. As a rule, Michelle responds to about half of them. Michelle remembers that one letter came in that looked normal, but after reading it she decided that people would send her anything. It read:

Dear Girl Scout Cookie People,

I'm writing to complain about the box that the cookies come in. Did you know that if you scrape the glue off the flaps that you can smoke it and get high? I think it is very irresponsible for the Girl Scouts to use glue in their cookie packaging. Please look into changing that for next year.

"Letters that sound threatening or kooky, I just put in the 'Freak File.' Those are the kind of letters that say things like, 'Girl Scouts is evil for killing the orangutan because they're killing all of the palm trees in Sumatra.' It's like, okay there's nothing I could say that would please you. Really we still get a small percentage of complaints. But the complaints we get show that these people have way too much time on their hands. I mean there's one thing if you're complaining about the quality of a product. It's another thing because they're blaming you for the deforestation in Brazil."

To get a bigger picture of what's going well with the cookie program, and to solve any big challenges, the senior staff brought together a Marketing Communications or "Mar-Com" network in which the councils work with the headquarter staff to solve difficult problems. Michelle is one of the lead people in the cookie group. These groups come up with materials that are updated every year. There's only an absolute overhaul every two to three years.

In 2005, the cookie bakeries, ABC Interbake and Little Brownie Bakers, reduced the trans fats in the cookies, so now there's zero trans fats per serving. The cookie buyers noticed the change, but they didn't always welcome it. Carts full of letters were dumped on Michelle's desk that protested the new taste that came with the new recipe. On the other side were the nutritionists who applauded the Girl Scout's decision to make a healthier product, but they too criticized the group because the no trans fats claim was only true when the consumer stuck to eating only the stated serving size and sometimes that serving size was only one cookie. Now all of the varieties are "zero trans fats free" per serving.

"The problem is that [our changes] are not good enough for some of the people," Michelle says. "They want trans fats free. And the problem is that we...it's a semantics war now between "zero trans fats" and "trans fats free." And our argument now is "Take it up with the FDA."

"It was the bane of our existence," Michelle reports. "So the Mar-Com cookie group had to put that information in their materials, and send it to everybody on the cookie team, and then send it to everybody else in the free world who works here." Michelle has limited patience for this kind of debate. This discussion has been going on for more than two years, and she finds it hard to keep coming up with new statements that will satisfy such cookie complaints. "These are cookies, for goodness sake. They're a treat. They're to be had in moderation. They're not to be eaten by the sleeve. Cookies in moderation are not bad. The cookies themselves do not make people fat. People make people fat."

❧

The Girl Scouts of the USA National Headquarters occupies nine floors in a New York office building at Thirty-Seventh Street and Fifth Avenue. The space, once used by Ted Turner for offices of Turner Broadcasting, now holds more than 300 staff members who keep the national programs going. Juliette Low, founder of the Girl Scouts, chose New York as the group's Headquarters just a few years after the organization began in her hometown of Savannah, Georgia, in 1912. Low moved the group to Washington, DC, for a short time while she sought national presence for the new organization, and then made the move to New York.

When I visited on a beautiful early spring day in midtown Manhattan in March 2009, not a trace of Girl Scout green was part of the décor throughout the beige maze of cubicles and office rooms. As visitors come into the large glass front doors of the Headquarters reception area, they notice the oversized framed beauty shots of Girl Scouts on the walls.

In addition to the politicians, industry leaders, and others who come to work with the Headquarters staff on Girl Scout business, thousands of Brownie, Junior, Cadette, and Senior Scouts come from all across the United States to visit the National Headquarters annually. The eager girls meet their official guide, pile into the first elevator that arrives, and are escorted to the top floor to take a tour in the Girl Scout Museum.

The museum, which takes up about a third of the seventeenth floor, is curated by the National Historic Preservation Center. Guides pass out a museum brochure at the first exhibit, which explains each historic Girl Scout artifact. A worn copy of the original Girl Scout handbook, *Scouting for Girls,* sits safely inside a glass cabinet, along with a Girl Scout doll from 1919, dressed in a khaki-colored uniform. Most Scouts are amused to see an original Brownie beanie on display. The pointed tip on the faded cap has a little bell sewn onto it, and a hand-painted Brownie on the front. A collection of uniforms shows the evolution of the Scout image. From the long stiff Brownie uniform of the 20s to the mini-dress-inspired uniform of the 70s to the comfortable pants and vests that present day Scouts are familiar with, the uniforms exhibit reflects the fashion taste of each generation.

The last stop on the museum tour is a small theater space where Scouts can watch a silent movie. With tinkling of piano music and captions telling the story, the black-and-white movie shows a group of Girl Scouts as they "save the day." Even though the show is in sharp contrast to the widescreen theaters that most girls are used to, they pile into the small theater, absorbed by the timeless story of girl ingenuity.

Yevgeniya Gribov is the Girl Scout archivist who makes certain that the most delicate antique uniforms and other memorabilia are protected from little hands. As she receives new donations, she adds new books and badges to the exhibit. A petite energetic woman, Yevgeniya has worked in the New York Headquarters archives for over a decade, since she moved to the United States from Russia. Although most of her time is spent cataloguing rows and rows of shelves filled with documents, she welcomes all visitors to the museum and she's always interested in the questions that girls ask.

"Just the other day a girl from Pittsburgh asked where Girl Scouts in the 20s put their cell phones. I had to tell her that they didn't have mobile phones back then," she said. "But most of the girls are happy to know that, almost from the beginning of Girl Scouts, there have been cookie sales."

While hundreds of young visitors skip through the museum each month, Michelle only bumps into any of them if, by chance, she happens upon an elevator full of Brownies or Cadettes. And although she is constantly quoted on television news programs and in newspapers across the country, she seldom leaves her office. Almost all of her work is done at her computer and on her Blackberry. Before the peanut butter recall became the focus of her cookie spin, stories about the bad economy, the shrinking size of the cookies, and the number of cookies in each box had been the focus of the reporters she talked to during the fall sale.

NEW YORK (CNN) – Eating a box of Girl Scout Cookies in one sitting will be a little bit easier this year: The Girl Scouts of the USA confirmed Wednesday that it has reduced the number of cookies per box to save money because of rising transportation and baking costs. People buying Girl Scout cookies like these on their Web site this year can expect fewer cookies in the packages.

From her first day on the job, there had been grumbling from customers about the number of cookies in each box, but this was the first year that Michelle had had a blitz of media calls on the size of the cookie itself. Her team met and came up with some talking points to counter this negative PR:

- The cost of baking a cookie today is significantly higher than it was even a year ago, and the bakers cannot continue to absorb these rising costs.
- Transportation costs have increased 30 to 40 percent from a year ago.
- The combined cost increase prompted the organization to "lower the net weight of our cookie boxes slightly rather than ask our customers to pay a higher per-package price during these difficult times."

Still, she had to concede that there were two to four fewer cookies in boxes of Thin Mints, Tagalongs, Samoas, Do-Si-Dos, and Trefoils.

The other news story that didn't seem to go away was how the taste of the cookies had somehow changed. The cookies that buyers had remembered from their youth seemed to be just a little off. When reporters called with that one, Michelle sighed with resignation as she had to set the record straight one more time.

"I keep having to tell people that the cookies are not the same," she says, "if they come from a different baker."

Until a recent reorganization of the Girl Scout councils, most customers could happily buy the cookie that they were used to. With the reorganization, which took several councils and put them together into one larger council, those who craved Peanut Butter Patties were being delivered boxes of Tagalongs and those who were used to savoring a stack of Trefoils with their morning coffee were dunking a handful of Shortbreads.

"There's a Girl Scout cookie myth," Michelle says, "that we have a Thin Mint recipe in a vault. We don't. We also don't have girls in the basement. The bakers come up with recipes. Bakers have been making Thin Mints since, I think, 1935. But when they are licensed with us, each baker comes up with their own recipe. Growing up, I was partial to Samoas. So when I first tried the Caramel deLites, I thought 'I don't like this.' But there's that nostalgia of youth. If it's not quite the same, it makes you angry because you want to have that feeling associated with your childhood."

Still, Girl Scout cookie buyers complain about this taste difference. As the "new" cookies make their way to consumers, the newspapers and blogs are full of protests like the following comment in which this consumer rationalizes about her council's switch from Samoas to Caramel deLites:

*In the continuing dumbing down of America, I would
guess that the Girl Scouts decided that their cookie
names were either too complicated or too foreign
sounding. And having not had a Girl Scout cookie in a
very long time, I noticed that the "Caramel deLites"
were not nearly as good as they were when I was a
Girl Scout myself. At least they've left the Thin Mint
alone: those are two words that are easy to pronounce!*

Another blogger talks about the differences that she's noticed in the two cookies:

*Samoas have dark chocolate, and more of it, more
caramel and coconut, and the cookie base has flavor.
Caramel deLites have waxy, fake-tasting milk
chocolate, with barely any caramel and coconut, and
the cookie base tastes like sawdust. Wish I could
describe it better...Maybe if I never tasted Samoas,
Caramel deLites would be adequate.*

Every summer, the Fifth Avenue Girl Scout Headquarters
becomes the site of a cookie "sit down" between the two
bakers. For hours, at least a half dozen representatives
from both ABC Interbake and Little Brownie Bakers sit
around the Girl Scouts conference table to hash out the
details of the upcoming year's cookie sale. Michelle recalls
that at 9:00 a.m. sharp, "taxis full of guys in suits" arrive,
and each team is kept separate until the group sits down
with the Girl Scouts senior staff. From there they work
out the program themes for the educational materials, any
new cookies to be added to the list of the traditional favorites, and even the color of the cookie boxes.

"In one meeting, the reps were getting really loud about the Trefoil/Shortbread boxes," Michelle says. "Grown men were shouting 'I want a lemon-colored box!' 'I want a custard-color box!' For me, yellow is yellow. But it took almost an hour until they were happy with the box colors."

As I found out for myself when I tried to visit a cookie facility, neither bakery allows visitors inside of their plants. ABC's public relations person points to the September 11 attacks and the possibility of terrorists as the reason to keep anyone but cleared workers away from the cookie manufacturing. Even top Girl Scout representatives must have a good reason to come in and no cameras are allowed.

"We don't even have any B-roll of the factories," Michelle says. "They keep promising 'next year,' but that never seems to happen. There's going to be some blood at the national cookie meeting this summer. Six hours with the cookie reps is going to make for good television."

When a new cookie flavor debuts, councils that order cookies from that bakery get promotional materials to give to the troops so that the girls will be able to answer questions about the new cookie during the early part of the sale. The baker also sends sample cookies to councils so that they can pass them along. Usually new types of cookies sell fairly well; as a rule, the biggest seller, Thin Mints, makes up 30 percent of sales; Samoa/Caramel deLites, 20 percent, the rest of the established cookies, 15 to 20 percent each. New cookie brands usually make up 10 percent of the troops' orders.

The year that Little Brownie Bakers introduced the self-named Little Brownie cookie, they had great expectations for the treat. What made this cookie different from those that came before was that the square crunchy chocolate treat was sugar-free *and* fat-free. As cartons of the cookies were shipped out from the factory on trucks, the bakers thought that they might have created a bestseller, hoping that this new option would allow people who generally pass on baked goods for health or nutritional reasons to finally be able to indulge in cookies. After the first batch of cookies were delivered, reports about the Little Brownie cookie weren't good. Kids didn't like it. Adults didn't like it. Not even the elderly or diabetic folks liked it. Except for cookies that the Girl Scout troops had already ordered, none of the waiting cartons were moving out of the plants.

Quality products and customer satisfaction, not surprisingly, are important to the Girl Scouts—after all, the cookie sale funds about 70 percent of the council level activities and close to 100 percent of troop activities. So maintaining a solid reputation is key to the organization's survival. After every year's sale, the National Office conducts a cookie audit for quality and customer satisfaction. If there's a year where they get more customer complaints than others—as with the Little Brownie cookie—then they get to the bottom of it and find out why. The audit is two-fold. It looks at the product itself, judging the quality of the product, and at the number of complaints and where they're located. For example, if there were a thousand more cookie complaints in the Pacific Northwest than anywhere else, they try to find out why. Has the facility changed? Have the cookies been lying around or kept in poor condition?

The audit that year showed only one thing about the Little Brownie. It just didn't taste good. How could this happen? Like most food manufacturers, Little Brownie Bakers held focus groups that told them the cookie was a viable product.

"It's really the best example to the girls about a business when something doesn't work than when it does," Michelle says. "Then you can see people didn't want it so it's not back. It explains the laws of supply and demand.

You don't want it; we're not going to give it to you. But you can't pull it off mid-season. They went through focus groups and people said that they liked the Little Brownie cookie, but I imagine that none of our focus groups did a test saying 'Here's a Samoa, here's a Trefoil, and here's the new sugar-free, fat-free caramelized dog poo. Which of these do you want?' I'm pretty sure that they probably just tested various flavors of the caramelized dog poo."

❧

I think this is more of an avocation than just a regular job. I think it does call to some people, and I think you have a probably higher percentage of women here [at the National Office] who were Girl Scouts growing up than in the general population...and studies show that approximately 80 percent of business leaders anywhere were Girl Scouts.

—Michelle Tompkins

In 2008, the Girl Scouts hired a new face to represent them in official marketing efforts. Laurel Richie, a stylish successful African American advertising executive who created campaigns for Campbell Soup, American Express, Oscar Mayer, Maidenform, and Kimberly-Clark became the group's first Senior Vice President and Chief Marketing Officer for the Girl Scouts. In her new job, she oversees the media and communications strategy. At Kimberly-Clark, Laurel helped update the Kotex brand for the twenty-first-century young woman, and the Girl Scouts are hoping that she can help attract "a new generation of girls and adult volunteers to the Girl Scout Movement."

While growing up in Tennessee in the 70s, Laurel and her sisters were Girl Scouts, and their mom handled the troop cookie orders. Looking back on her long history with the organization, the new PR maven says that the group's image is still stuck in an earlier time. Without a more modern version of Girl Scouts to engage twenty-first-century girls, the organization can't hope to compete with the new digital world. That image predicament is what Laurel thinks may explain why the Girl Scouts have had an 8 percent drop in membership in the past 10 years.

"It's no different from preparing an ad campaign for a classic brand that needs a bit of a facelift to show that it's still relevant," Laurel said in a *Washington Post* article called "Badges Out, Blogs In as Girl Scouts Modernize." In an effort to make Girl Scouts more contemporary, Laurel has set her agenda this way:

"The Girl Scouts will continue its long-standing traditions of camping, hiking, and community service, but it also is promoting programs that help build self-esteem and encourage healthy living choices."

Her arrival and ideas have been welcomed by most, especially when she assured everyone that the cookie sales would continue, but one long-standing Girl Scout supporter posted her thoughts questioning the direction of the group under Laurel's leadership on the *girlscout.org* Web site:

The focus of the program has simply changed too much over the last five years or so for many of us. As a home-schooling, stay-at-home mom, who was very successful in the business world, I know better than anyone just how many forms 'leadership' can take and Girl Scouts seems to be rather limited in their view.

NEW YORK, N.Y. —Neither licensed baker affiliated with Girl Scout® Cookies ABC Interbake and Little Brownie Bakers source their peanut butter from the supplier involved in the current peanut butter warning. FDA and other regulatory agencies have indicated that Peanut Corporation of America (PCA) is the focus of their investigation concerning a recent Salmonella outbreak thought to be caused by tainted peanut butter. PCA does not supply peanut butter used in any variety of Girl Scout® cookies. Food safety and quality are of the utmost importance to us. The Girl Scout® Cookie Program is the nation's premier entrepreneurship and educational program for girls and we appreciate your support in your local communities.

On Day Six of the Peanut Butter Crisis, after Laurel gave the official press release her blessing, Michelle sent it out to the media and all of the council offices. Although the salmonella scare brought the sale of snack crackers and other peanut butter products to a new low, early reports from the councils say that orders for Do-Si-Dos/Peanut Butter Sandwich cookies and Tagalongs/Peanut Butter Patties were still strong. But the next few months will tell the full story.

Meanwhile, there's always breaking news about cookies for Michelle to deal with.

"I thought I would end up back in LA working in the industry. I didn't think I'd be a publicist. I thought I'd be a journalist. I still have ambitions to write, but right now anything beyond a press release is beyond my mental capabilities at the end of the day."

Michelle thinks about the days to come and decides there is a definite possibility that she will someday move back to California.

"I thought I wanted to do one year in the city after being a student, and one year turned into two and then three. I just don't think I'm going to make the rule of becoming a New Yorker...I don't think I'll be here for 10 years. I like California," she confides. "In the end, it's going to win. I hate the summers in New York. They are cruel and unusual punishment. I'm from Sacramento—give me 120 degrees and no humidity, but this 80 degrees with 80 percent humidity is not going to cut it for much longer."

With that, she turns to her Blackberry to check for the next big story that would need her spin. ❧

"I joined the Brownies in 1957, as soon as I turned seven years old. Although I don't remember what year it was–sometime between 1958 and 1961–I do remember that one year the cost of cookies went from 25 to 35 cents a box. This was significant because we all had to learn to make change, beyond just giving people quarters!"

Martha Moore

RETIRED GIRL SCOUT COOKIE FLAVORS—GONE BUT NOT FORGOTTEN

Chocoroons
Almond Swirls
Butter Nut Roundups
Savannahs
Pixies
Iced Oatmeal
Kokos
Frostee Twists
Icebox Cookies
Dutch Dainties
Apricot Flippettes
Lemon Lime Cremes
Coconut
Sesame Crisps
Swiss Chalet
Snaps
Chedarettes
Sugar and Spice
Van'chos
Snowdrop
Sugar Wafers
Health Cookies
Gauchos
Sherbert Cremes

Lemon Coolers
Ice Berry Piñatas
Custard
Golden Nut Clusters
Trail Mix
Pecan Nut
Cabana Cremes
Country Hearth Chips
Lemonades
Echo Cookies
Chocolate Chunk
Pecan Shortees
Forget-Me-Nots
Apple Cinnamons
Choc. Chip Granola
Ole-Ole
Aloha Chips
Molasses
Animal Treasures
Medallions
Short Teas
Lemon Chip
Little Brownies
Cinnaspins

Classic Cookie Match-ups

D epending on where you live and the baker that your council buys cookies from, you may be biting into a Caramel deLite or munching on a Samoa. And although they may look pretty much the same, even Thin Mints are cookie cousins rather than twins. That's because both bakers have developed unique recipes (or formulas, as they say in the cookie manufacturing business) for the five customer favorite cookie varieties.

Recently, I had the chance to eat cookies like the other half does. Since my council has commissioned cookies from Little Brownie for years, I had no idea how ABC Baker's cookies tasted. There indeed were subtle taste differences, but I was pleased to discover how delicious the cookies were. From this unofficial taste test, I can confirm that no matter where you live in the United States, your cookie is a winner!

ABC Bakers	Little Brownie Bakers
Thin Mints	Thin Mints
Caramel deLites	Samoas
Shortbreads	Trefoils
Peanut Butter Sandwich	Do-Si-Dos
Peanut Butter Patties	Tagalongs

Cookies on Ice

I n the shadow of the gently rolling Shenandoah Mountains of Virginia, about an hour from the White House and the United States Capitol, is a lesser-known large white building where another symbol of Americana is said to be born. Actually making your way to the sprawling compound requires careful navigation—there are no tourist maps to guide those who dare to make the trip. GPS wouldn't help either; directions to the desired destination are not in Siri's data banks. The journey is as fraught with twists and wrong turns as any expert hiking trail. Yes, for me, finding one of the few factories that is rumored to bake and ship millions of boxes of delectable Girl Scout cookies required preparation, resourcefulness, and persistence; all traits of a good Scout.

Moving no faster than the 25 mile per hour speed limit posted on the back roads of the small Virginia town near the factory, I drove with steady resolve as my husband, Tony, rode shotgun in our silver minivan. Also along for the adventure were my niece, Monica, and puppy, Daisy. To the casual observer, we looked like an innocent group out for a Sunday drive in the country.

For months I'd tried to arrange a legitimate tour through the factory, but I never received any answers to my email or voicemail requests. I'd even broached the subject with the Girl Scouts National Headquarters Spokesperson when I met with her in New York, but she put the total kibosh on my dreams to actually see the inner workings of the plant where the legendary cookies are made.

"Nobody gets in," she told me. It seemed to be a matter of national security. After all, what would happen if a terrorist got access to the cookies? "Just watch the episode of 'Unwrapped,' where they show other cookie manufacturing," she suggested. "You'll get the basic idea." I left the interview feeling discouraged. If the National Office couldn't (or wouldn't) give me access to the cookie factories, who could? I decide to work with Girl Scout ingenuity to solve this dilemma.

As most cookies lovers know, for the past decade or so, there have been only two bakers licensed to make Girl Scout cookies. Little Brownie Bakers, headquartered in Lexington, Kentucky, has been making cookies since 1975. It is a subsidiary of Keebler, known for their cookie-baking elves, which is owned by Kellogg's. ABC Bakers, which has been making cookies for the Scouts since 1939, is headquartered in Richmond, Virginia, and is a subsidiary of Interbake, owned by George Weston Ltd. Although there are subtle taste differences between cookies made by the two bakeries, only Thin Mints share a common name.

In 2006, ABC built a modern baking facility in Front Royal, Virginia, and moved that end of their operation from Richmond, which began under the name of Southern Biscuit Works in 1900, to the new site. And it was to that bastion of cookies that our Sunday adventure led us. To get a fuller sense of the story of Girl Scout cookies and to be able to tell the story as well as possible, I was determined to at least catch a glimpse of the factory.

The address for the factory was listed on the Internet as Baker Plaza, but that street name couldn't be found through MapQuest, Google Maps, or Rand McNally. For a while, it seemed that the secret location of the factory would thwart my efforts. In a moment of inspiration, I queried ABC Bakers and Front Royal on Yahoo and came up with a useful hit. A 2007 municipal report that documented the construction of the new factory gave the original name of the street where the new factory had been built. ABC had changed the name from Bering Plaza to Baker Plaza.

On our trip to the factory, my eyes swept to the left and then to the right of the two-lane-road for any clues that we were going in the right direction. Since it was the weekend, there was no traffic coming toward us or behind us. After passing over a line of railroad tracks—a landmark we'd seen that was close to the cookie plant—anticipation began to build. Any moment now, we'd be at the factory. I spotted the street sign for Baker Plaza and pulled the car off the road and parked in front of a heavily gated entrance. We sat in the car for what seemed like an hour, but it was actually less than a minute. What was our plan? Should we get out? Was anyone in the guard's booth? At that close distance, in front of the gently waving US, Canadian, and Interbake Bakery flags, we could read the sign posted for all to see:

Private Property—No Trespassing. No Photography.

Tony and Monica jumped out of the car to see if they could get any closer. I stayed behind the wheel with the engine running. As they walked toward the gate, a guard came out of the booth. She didn't look particularly menacing, but they froze in place when they spotted her.

"Can I help you?" she asked. Her gray uniform stretched and wrinkled in all of the wrong places, and although she had what appeared to be a pistol at her side, I doubted she'd ever had to use it. Her puzzled expression told us that she wasn't accustomed to visitors coming to the plant on the weekend. I imagined that we'd interrupted her watching a tear jerker of a chick flick on her smartphone, and she was ready to get back to that drama, instead of ours.

"We just needed to stretch our legs," Monica said. She moved back toward the car. Tony stood waiting for the woman to respond.

"Sorry, you can't stop here. We don't allow visitors."

"Any chance we could walk our dog for a moment?" Tony pointed to our little pup as a last ditch effort to buy more time. Paranoia began to set in, and I wondered if my tags were being run by an unseen second guard to determine whether we were terrorists who were there to destroy the cookies. Could the three of us—all middle-aged folks who looked like they'd had more than their shares of Girl Scout cookies—and a sweet little dog really look like radicals? I decided not to find out.

"No problem," I said to her from my open window. "Let's go. We'll stop somewhere else." Tony and Monica were trying to help me get some inside information for my project, but I didn't want us to land in jail for trespassing. They climbed into the car and we drove down the street and turned left into the next driveway. This one didn't have any guards or signs. We got out of the car and laughed. Our big adventure had lasted for all of five minutes.

From across the road we got a better look at the Interbake factory, and we took a few photos to remember our cookie caper. The plant building reminded me of a penitentiary. A long white single-story plant stretched almost the length of land it sat on. Massively tall fences, like those I'd seen once on a college field trip to a women's prison, surrounded the property. The only thing missing from the Interbake fence was barbed wire. Those cookies within were on lockdown, and they had no chance for an early parole.

By the time we left, the sun had set and we headed back to a nearby mall to get some pizza before getting back on the highway. Although I hadn't had the chance to discover any classified secrets during our brief visit, I left feeling pretty good. And we all slept a little sounder that night, knowing that Girl Scout cookies are safe from any lurking security threats. ✤

"Back when I was selling Girl Scout cookies in my home-town, there was a very old house that was hidden in the woods and the other girls were too afraid to ring the door-bell because they thought the house was haunted. One day I summoned up my courage and rang the bell. A silver-haired lady, who must have been at least 90 and was real-ly nice, answered. After I gave my sales spiel, she asked to see the order form. She held a magnifying glass over the glossy color photos and got a good look at all of the cook-ies. Then she ordered at least 20 boxes—paid for later in cash–which she said she would keep fresh in the freezer. Because she couldn't see well, she asked me to fill out the form for her. Being a good Girl Scout, I was happy to help her in any way I could.

Lisa McPherson

"My Daisy troop learned a valuable lesson about reaching out to all cookie customers—even if there is a language barrier. One day we were at our local bowling alley where we set up a cookie booth in the lobby. After a while, another group of people came in to set up their own tables to sell non-cookie products. My girls asked those at the other table if they wanted to buy cookies but made no sales. The young Girl Scouts grew increasingly frustrated because they thought they were being ignored. When they told me about it, I took notice and realized that the people in the other group were actually deaf. They weren't ignoring the girls; they simply couldn't hear them. Thanks to my smartphone, I was able to quickly look up 'American Sign Language,' which allowed the girls to sign the word 'cookie' with their verbal sales pitch. That definitely got people's attention! Later on, the woman in charge of the other group came up and showed them how to sign Girl Scout cookie. We combined that with the little sign language I knew so the girls could tell customers (in sign language) 'my favorite Girl Scout cookie is' and they would point. We ended up selling many more boxes that day simply because we made an effort to include everybody and communicate using their language."

Christy Hepburn

The Last Cookie in the Sleeve

You know how it happens. You rip open a box of Thin Mints (or fill in your favorite Girl Scout cookie here) and after satisfying crunchy blitz, too quickly you reach for the last cookie in the sleeve. If you're like me, you're surprised that the end has come so soon. Then you take a breath, pop the final cookie in your mouth, and savor the goodness. For me, writing this afterword is somewhat like coming to the last cookie. Although the end has almost come, I have the chance to look back at my Girl Scout cookie project with appreciation.

The idea of creating a tribute to the Girl Scout cookie program was born in 2007, during my first summer residency at the Goucher College Creative Nonfiction MFA program. When I applied to the program, I was terrified of becoming a student again, but I knew that I had to do it. Despite my anxieties, I was ready to tackle the daunting task of writing a book. So one blistering August morning when my writing mentor issued her challenge to write about our own brand of high school geekdom, I did a high dive into the deep end of my memories and surfaced with a Thin Mint. When I read my scribbled Girl Scout cookie sales remembrances, I could tell that the subject matter resonated with my classmates. The former Girl Scouts in the room began sharing their own stories, and the guys reminisced about eating their favorite cookies.

I left the residency with the "cookie book" as just one of a few ideas, but for the next few months I kept coming back to it. In November, after committing to this thesis, I began to look for a troop that would be willing to let me shadow them during their sales season. Jennifer M. (I did not disclose her last name in this book to protect her daughters' privacy) was not only open to the idea, she was welcoming. At the first meeting I attended, most of the girls in her troop were chatty and charming but some eyed me with suspicion and a few ignored me completely. Eventually, however, all of the girls warmed up to me and my ever-present notebook and digital recorder. The troop members who, at that time, were in middle and high school are now beautiful poised college students who are using many of the skills they gained as Girl Scouts in their studies on campuses throughout the United States.

Besides doing research as to what happens on the troop level, I also sought to gain a broader base of knowledge about cookie sale logistics. To get a better sense of that process, I went wherever I could to get "insider" information, which included attending a regional cookie manager training, helping to unload more than a million cookies from a moving van (where I got hit on by the van driver), making multiple bus trips to New York City to conduct research at the Girl Scouts' archives, and flying to Houston, Texas, in November 2011 to attend the Girl Scout convention that celebrated the group's centennial year. Years after my caper to find the Interbake factory, I discovered that Girl Scout cookies are actually baked in South Dakota, but I was assured that the facility is much like the Virginia bakery that I visited and described in the "Cookies on Ice" chapter.

In all of these places and at every event I met friendly women who generously shared their experiences with me. There were even a few kind Girl Scout staff members who shared information with me twice—first when I was writing my thesis and more recently when I was updating information for this publication. So, although I was the one who transcribed multiple interviews and wrestled with finding the right creative phrasing, this is not just my book. It is the compilation of stories told by Girl Scouts from many places and generations. While the details disclosed in this book were learned by observing one troop in Maryland, their activities and accomplishments are typical of past and present Girl Scout troops across the nation. Through this venerable organization, girls from all walks of life learn skills and have experiences that will serve them throughout their lives. As one of my friends who never had the chance to be a Girl Scout said after reading this book, "I never knew what I missed!" ❧

Made in the USA
Charleston, SC
09 December 2016